746.44

WITHDRAWN

Edges and Finishes
in Machine Embroidery

Edges and Finishes in Machine Embroidery

Valerie Campbell-Harding

B T BATSFORD

First Published 2004

Text and diagrams © Valerie Campbell-Harding 2004

Volume © B T Batsford

Photography unless specified otherwise (VCH: Valerie
Campbell-Harding) by Michael Wicks

ISBN 07134 8867 0

A CIP catalogue record for this book is available from
the British Library.

Printed in Malaysia

for the publishers
B T Batsford
Chrysalis Books Group
The Chrysalis Building
Bramley Road
London W10 6SP

www.batsford.com

A member of **Chrysalis** Books plc

Acknowledgements

Many thanks to:

The colleagues and students who have lent such
stunning pieces to be photographed for this book

Michael Wicks for his wonderful photography.

Illustration page 1: Bustier with piped seams, lacy edges
worked on water-soluble fabric and ruffles edged with
automatic stitch patterns. (Elli Woodsford)

Illustration page 2: Stiff bag with curved edges, richly
stitched, and buttonholed and beaded rings.
(Flower)

Illustration page 3: Samples of many different edges,
bound, stitched, burnt and beaded.

Illustration left: Beaded book with zigzagged cords with
Peyote stitched ends. (Gill Morgan)

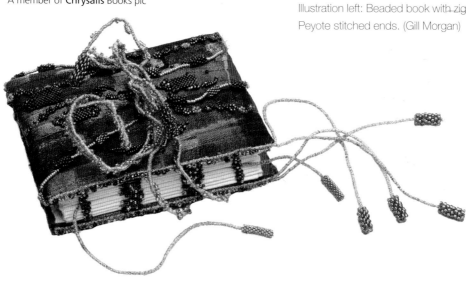

CONTENTS

INTRODUCTION

The importance of edges and finishings

Almost every piece of embroidery, quilting or soft furnishing needs some form of finishing or edging – maybe just a simple hem or binding but more often a truly decorative finishing that enhances the textile. So often these finishing techniques are an afterthought, but they should be designed when the textile is designed, and should use the same style of stitching, and, often, the same threads or fabrics.

The edges and finishes in this book are designed for machine embroidery, and the methods given would cover wall hangings and panels, books, bags, vessels, bowls, belts, lampshades, cushions and many other pieces. The scale of the cords, braids and other techniques in this book can be tiny or giant, made from different materials than those suggested, and used differently, but they must be suitable for their purpose.

Any modern sewing machine will do all the stitching suggested here, but you will find that you need some feet that do not come with the machine. Extra feet can be bought for any make of machine, but may have to be ordered from the retailer. It is worth buying feet specially made for the purpose, as they make the job so much easier and save time and hassle. When you have decided which of the techniques to try, have a look at the feet on the opposite page to see what you will need.

Right: Small wrap-around book cover made from woven strips of embroidery with burnt edges, decorated with leather thong giving a fringed edge.

What feet to use

Some useful feet already come with your machine. Others it is well worth going out to buy, as they make the job so much easier. You may have to order them from your sewing machine dealer, but, believe me, it is worth the trouble and expense.

The ones I think are essential are:

1 The **satin stitch pattern** foot, also sometimes called the embroidery foot. This should already be in your box if you have a machine that does satin stitch patterns. There is extra space underneath the foot to allow the thicker stitching to go through easily, and the toes are wide apart so that you can see what you are stitching.

2 The **braiding** foot, also called the **'pearls and piping'** foot, or the **knit edge** foot. Whatever it is called, there is a tunnel underneath that allows you to zigzag over string or other cords, and it controls the string so that it does not leap about while you are stitching it. You can do machine-wrapped cords without a foot on at all, but it is more tiring and harder on your eyes.

3 The **overlock** foot allows you to stitch satin or zigzag stitches right on the edge of a fabric, with the stitches swinging over the metal bar on the right so that the fabric is not crumpled or distorted. Put the foot on your machine as usual, and lay the fabric underneath it with the edge of the fabric just under the bar.

4 The **edge stitch** foot allows you to stitch straight stitches right up to the edge of a fabric. Without this foot on, you might shred the fabric as you are stitching, and not be able to stitch as near the edge of it as you might wish.

All of these feet, as well as the standard foot and the **free embroidery, quilting** or **darning** feet, were used to work the samples and finished embroideries in this book.

Saving your back

A useful tip is to wedge something under the back of your sewing machine to tilt it forward slightly. This can be done using two spools of thread, or – much better – rubber door wedges. These are cheap and stable in use. I find that I do not then crouch forward to see what is being stitched, but immediately sit up straighter. Try it.

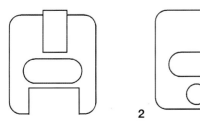

1

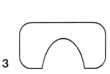

3

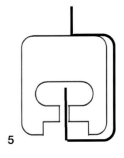

4 5

1 *Satin stitch pattern foot*
2 *Braiding foot*
3 *Underneath of braiding foot*
4 *Overlock foot*
5 *Edge stitch foot*

1 FABRIC EDGES

The simplest edge on a piece of fabric is a cut edge – but think instead of a torn, frayed or burnt edge, a folded, bound or piped edge, or a stitched edge. Each of these techniques gives a totally different character to the fabric and should be carefully considered at the design stage. Try some experiments on the fabrics before you finally decide, and always be prepared to change your mind.

Right: Panel with frayed strips of fabric on a painted fabric background, decorated with cable stitch. (Ruth Issett)

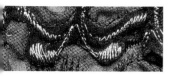

Cut edges

A beautifully cut edge is sharp, neat and uncomplicated. It cannot be done with every fabric, and cutting a smooth edge is an art. Often there are jaggies, or the shape is not perfect, but practice helps. Simple stitching shows this off well, but if the results are not as good as you wish they can always be covered with extra stitching.

Using large shears and cutting slowly and carefully gives a smooth edge, and pinking shears a toothed edge. This is visually strong and calls for a simple line of straight stitch to hold the shapes down.

Method

Fabrics

Use a smooth, fairly firm fabric such as felt, velvet, organza or good quality cotton. Soft, flimsy fabrics, or those with a texture, are often difficult to cut neatly.

Needle

Use a sewing machine needle to suit the fabric. A large needle, for example, might leave holes in fine silk or organdie.

Top thread

Work with machine embroidery thread, either coloured or metallic.

Bobbin thread

You can use a machine embroidery thread or a bobbin fill. If you have a metallic thread through your needle, do not use one on the bobbin – it will not show anyway. You can often use up oddments of threads that are already on some of your bobbins.

Tension

This should be normal – that is, the bobbin thread should not show on the top of the fabric. However, rules are made to be broken, and this could be a feature, with tiny loops of a different-coloured bobbin thread adding interest.

Foot

Use the standard foot for plain stitching, or a darning or free embroidery foot if you wish the stitching to be less regular and if you prefer this method.

Teeth

These should be up if you are using the standard foot, or down if you are doing free embroidery.

Stitch

Work in straight or free running stitch. When doing free running on edges, I like to work about three rows of stitching. You could also use a narrow satin stitch just inside the edge, rather than over it, allowing a small border of fabric to show.

Stitch length

This can be about $2\frac{1}{2}$ if you are using the standard foot. If you are using the free embroidery foot then the stitch length does not apply, as you control this by the speed at which you move the frame.

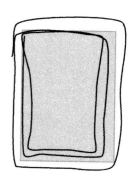

Above left: A piece of fabric applied with straight stitching worked with the foot on and the teeth up.

Above right: Fabric applied using straight stitching with the freehand embroidery foot and the teeth.

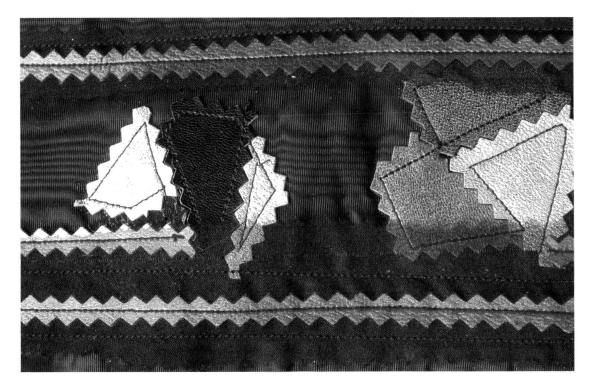

Left: Applied shapes cut with pinking shears.

Below: A large automatic pattern worked on black felt, cut out and then gently knotted. It was then applied to the backing made from orange silk, black net and the same pattern stitched in black. Heating with a gun melted some of the net, and the knotted strips were attached using free embroidery.

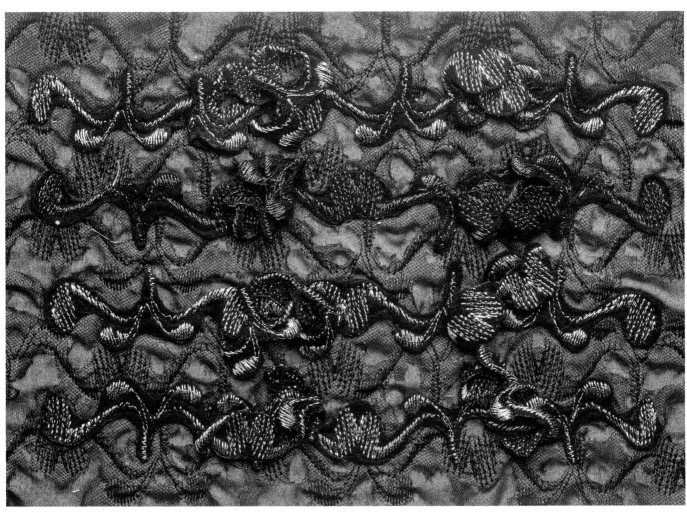

Right: Two bags, a cock and a hen, using frayed strips to give the feel of feathers. (Viv White)

Opposite: A seed head was dragged along a scanner to give this interrupted pattern with interesting edges, which was then carried out in black felt, coffee-dyed calico and machine stitching.

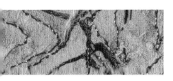

Torn edges

Torn edges are more informal than cut edges, and can be combined with fraying. Tearing paper is flexible as you can tear in any direction and around curved shapes, although the grain of the paper will give different results. Tearing fabric is more restricted as you can only tear along the grain, giving straight edges. Not all fabrics will tear and you will have to try each fabric to see what happens.

Having torn the edges, you can then leave them slightly curled, fray them by pulling threads away from the edge, or iron them flat, although you will lose some of the characteristics of the tearing.

The edges can be lightly stitched, or more heavily to hide them altogether if you wish. I like the stitching to be as invisible as possible so that you can see the texture of the fabric edge.

Opposite page: Tissue paper was stitched onto coffee dyed and stencilled calico using free running stitch. The paper was wetted and some rubbed away to give an interesting texture and gold paint was dabbed on.

Below: Frayed strips of organza were woven over the abstract butterfly shapes to give an interesting background. The shapes were then outlined and the strips attached with free machine embroidery.

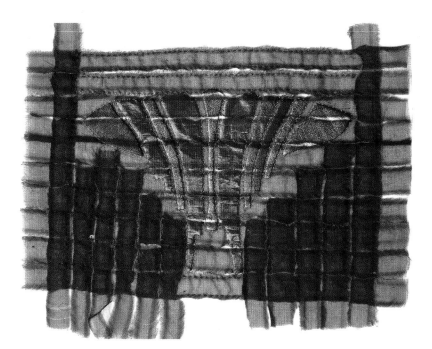

Method

Fabrics
The best fabrics to tear are the fine, smooth ones, but the fibre makes a difference. Silks can be good, and some synthetic fabrics, but heavily textured fabrics are usually impossible to tear. Any paper will tear, and most are easy to stitch on.

Needle
Use a needle that does not leave a mark on the fabric and is suitable for the thread you are using.

Top thread
Any machine embroidery thread can be used. You could use an invisible nylon monofilament if you want delicacy.

Bobbin thread
Use a machine embroidery thread or a bobbin fill.

Tension
Normal.

Foot
Either use a standard foot for straight stitching, or a free embroidery foot.

Teeth
These should be up if you are using the standard foot, or down if you are doing free embroidery.

Stitch
Work in straight or free running stitch.

Stitch length
This can be about 2½ if you are using the standard foot. If you are using the free embroidery foot then the stitch length does not apply as you control this by the speed at which you move the frame.

Right: A paper napkin, coloured with ink, was stitched in parallel lines. It was then wetted and rubbed to remove some of the paper, leaving interesting edges.

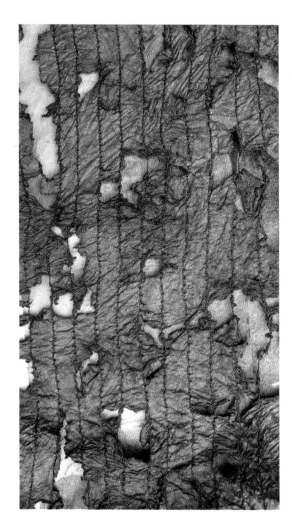

Far right: This was then laid on a painted fabric backing, with some scraps of painted tissue paper, and secured with long lines of straight stitch. The patterned shapes were worked separately and applied with free stitching afterwards.

Opposite page, bottom: A small panel with a background of torn scraps of silk paper, painted and printed. Torn stitched paper scraps were laid on top, some lengths of zigzagged cord applied, and small stiff 'bumps' of firm stitching on water-soluble fabric.

Below: A panel including some silk pods, wetted and peeled into thin layers, torn homemade silk paper, scraps of stitching, and some strips of paper napkin stitched in a grid pattern.

Burnt or melted edges

This gives you a lovely organic edge, seals any loose ends of threads, and can darken the colour of the fabric slightly to give more definition. On small pieces, the resulting stiffening is often an advantage.

Method

1 Any fabric will burn, but synthetic fabrics burn the most easily. I usually burn an edge after I have stitched it, to finish off the embroidery. There are several ways of doing this:

• You can cut shapes or seal edges using a fine-tipped soldering iron. Also, after cutting the edge, if you run the side of a hot iron along the edge you will melt and seal it without adding any colour or noticeable texture.

• You can hold the edge of the fabric in the side of a flame. I use a nightlight rather than a candle as it is more stable. Hold a piece of damp kitchen paper or a wet cloth in your hand while you are doing this, as some fabrics can catch fire and you will need to dab the fabric to put the flame out.

• You can use a mini blow-torch (the size of a long pencil) to seal the edges.

• You can use a joss stick, but I find it rather slow.

The best place to do this burning is on a draining board. Be careful that you do not have doors or windows open, nor your extractor fan switched on.

2 To burn irregular holes in a fabric after it has been stitched, the best tool to use is a heat gun which melts synthetic fabrics. This tool looks rather like a paint stripper but is less fierce, and you hold it near the place you wish to burn a hole. The longer you hold it in the same place, the larger the hole will be.

The business end of the heat gun gets very hot, so keep it away from you, and place it very carefully on its own stand to cool down.

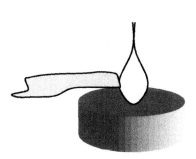

A piece of fabric held in a nightlight to burn the edges.

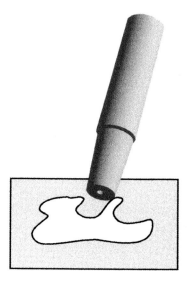

A heat gun used to partially melt man-made fabrics.

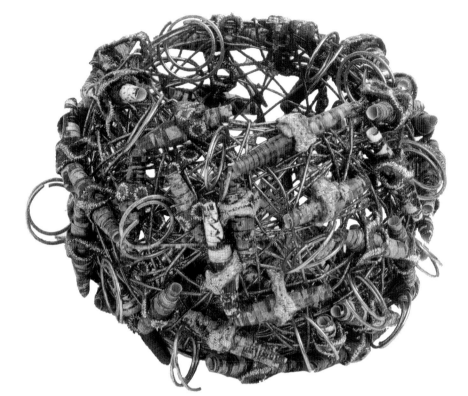

Left: A vessel made on a wire frame woven with cut out and burnt strips of an automatic pattern worked on felt, paper beads made from computer prints and wire spirals.

Below: A piece of paper was stitched using a twin needle to make ridges. It was wetted, partially rubbed away and the edges burnt on a nightlight. It was laid on blue organza, covered with a thin film of homemade silk paper and more pin tucks worked through all the layers.

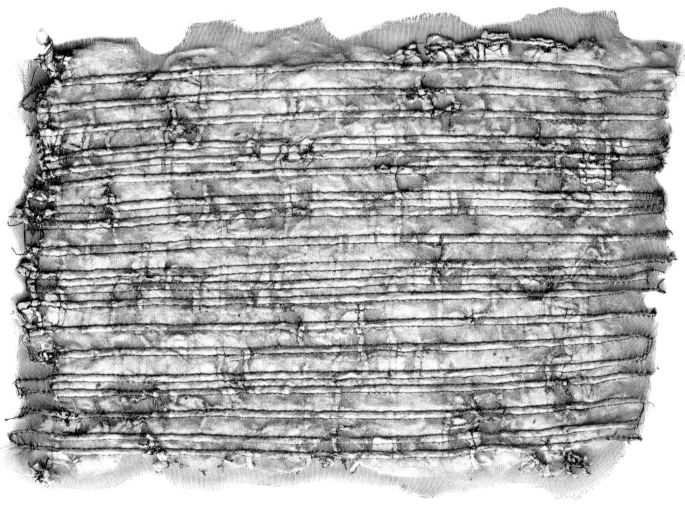

Strips of newspaper were laid on a calico backing, stitched and partially rubbed away. Chevrons of black felt and tissue paper bonded to felt were applied. A cream chiffon scarf was laid over the whole piece and more stitching worked to emphasise the pattern. This was partially melted using a heat gun.

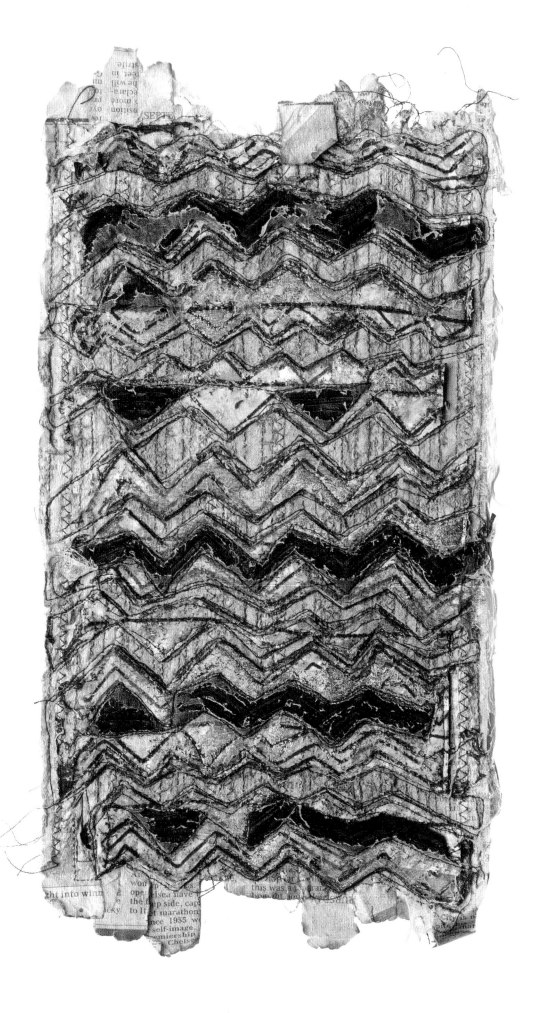

A richly stitched book used the same technique of partially melted chiffon to give texture, with a bookmark and strap using the same technique. (Cherry Thorne)

Right: A rolled bead made from a layered fabric shape outlined with an automatic machine pattern, the holes burnt with soldering iron. (Gill Morgan)

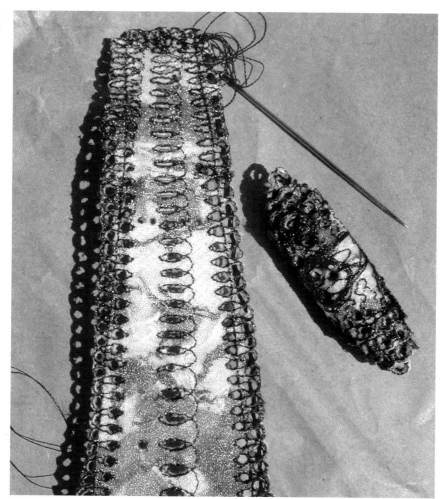

Below: Nylon chiffon was laid on a printed fabric. Previously stitched letters were cut out, the edges burnt and laid on top to make a border pattern. Extra stitching outlined the pattern and the chiffon was melted using a heat gun.

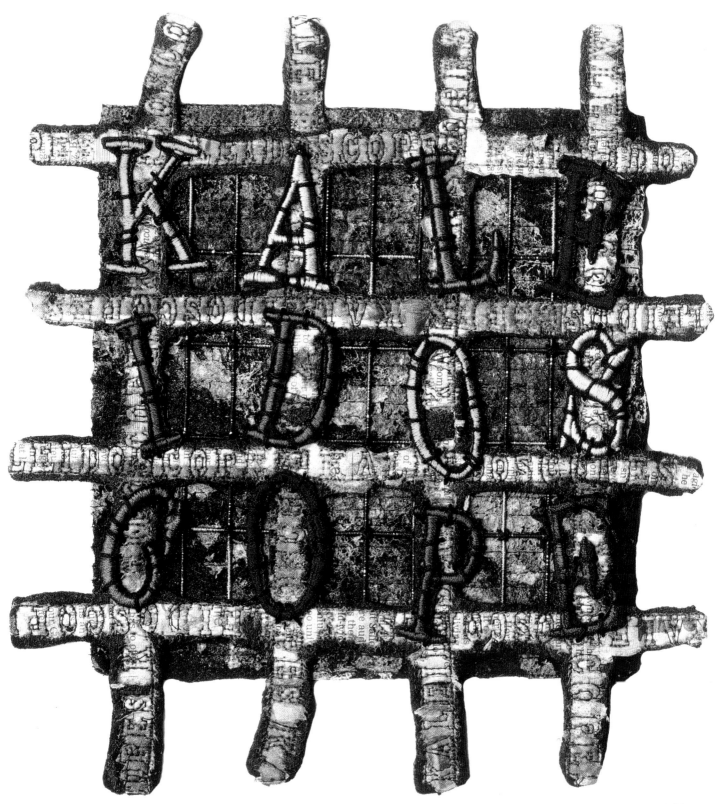

The background was made from silk-painted newspaper laid on felt, stitched, wetted and partially rubbed away. A metal grid was laid over it and stitched using a variegated thread. Another piece of newspaper fabric was made and stitched with the word 'kaleidoscope'. Holes and the edges were cut and burnt, and it was laid on top and stitched. The letters were stitched, cut out, burnt and stitched in place.

Bound edges

Right: The letter X was stitched on black net that was used to bind the edge. The net was melted away between the letters to give a shaped edge.

Raw edges that might be difficult to finish off any other way can be bound with another fabric, or the binding can be a purely decorative finish. The classic method of binding edges can be developed by using plain or patterned transparent fabrics, pre-embroidered fabrics using either automatic stitch patterns or free embroidery, or strips of lacy embroidery worked on water-soluble fabrics. They can be bound with commercial ribbons, raffia, strips of net or builders' scrim, or strips of solid embroidery worked for the purpose.

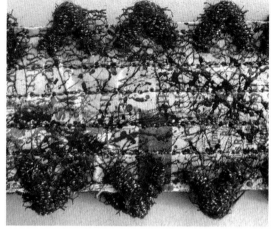

Method

The edging strip can be cut on the bias – necessary if the edge is a curve – or on the straight if the edge to be bound is also straight.

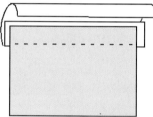

1 Place the fabric and binding right sides together and stitch them together, with the standard foot on and the teeth up, using a fairly small stitch, about length 2.

2 The edging strip is then turned to the back, a hem is folded under, and secured by hand or machine. This is another opportunity to use some sort of decorative stitching.

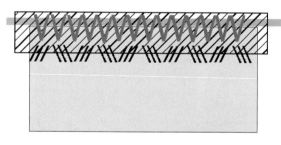

Top: The basic method for a bound edge.
Bottom: Binding an edge with a transparent fabric

Right: A sample showing a bound edge using previously stitched net.

A bag made from sections of painted stitched silk and paper, bound in the same way as the top sample on p. 24. The corners were curled over beads made from rolled and melted nappy liner and wire, and knotted tassels were added to the points. (See p. 104 for how to make these tassels.)

Points and tabs

Flaps and tabs make a wonderful edge on many articles, especially cushions, clothing and bags. They can be made of the same fabric as the main embroidery, or from a different one. The fabric can be embroidered, pintucked or decorated with lengths of ribbon stitched on.

Triangular shapes can be made using narrow strips of fabric, ribbons or rouleaux. Short lengths are folded into a V shape and inserted into a seam. These can interlock along the edge.

Method

Tabs

Cut rectangles of fabric, twice as long as you wish the tabs to be, and add a normal seam allowance. The raw edges can be joined either by seaming them and turning the resulting tube inside out, or by folding the edges in and then stitching them down decoratively.

Below: A strip of fabric is folded in half and stitched. It is turned inside out, cut into shorter lengths and inserted into a seam.

Fold the tabs in half and lay them on the edge of the embroidery with the bottom edges level with the embroidered edge. Lay the second piece of embroidery, or another piece of fabric, over the top and stitch together. Fold the fabrics back, exposing the tabs.

Prairie points

This is an old technique which uses rectangles of fabric folded in half along the length, then the two top corners are folded in so that the edges touch each other. These triangles can be interleaved, or inserted into a seam with just the points overlapping each other. The fun comes when the fabric is decorated beforehand, and this can be related to the main embroidery. The decoration can be complex, or just simple rows of stitching.

Shaped tabs

These can be cut from solid stitching or stitched especially for the purpose. It is best to use something firm, like felt, for the base – otherwise the tabs may be too floppy.

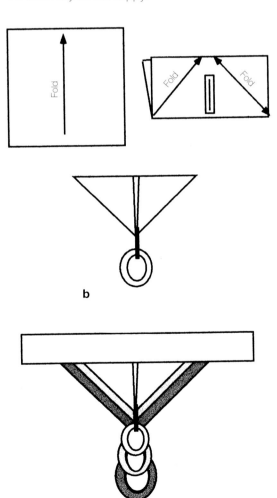

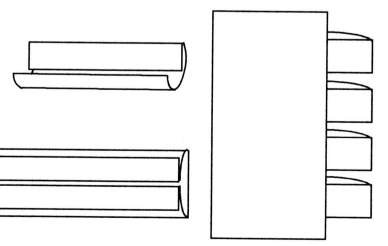

Above: Prairie Points made using a rectangle of fabric, folded, with a buttonhole worked in the centre of the fold from which to hang a tassel or wrapped rings.

Left: Heavily stitched pieces of fabric are applied to similar stitching.

Left: Prairie Points made from previously stitched calico.

Left: An intricate edge made from folded strips of stitching, bound with organza. Zigzagged cord was woven though to secure the folds and knotted with an overhand knot.

Pintucks and piping

Piping is a classic way of finishing a seamed edge. If the piping is decorated with pintucks, either worked solidly or with spaces between them, the results are truly impressive. Extra stitching can be added between the tucks, or narrow ribbons can be stitched down.

Method

Fabrics
Choose fairly soft, fine fabrics. Although velvet tucks beautifully, many other thick fabrics do not. You will just have to try a small sample.

Needle
Use a twin needle. These come in different sizes and the box is marked with two numbers. The first number gives the space between the needles, and the second number is the needle size. The smallest are used for materials such as organza, and the largest for velvet.

Top thread
Two threads are used, one through each needle. They can be different colours and different types of thread – for example, one thread coloured and one metallic.

You are sometimes instructed to put one thread on each side of the tension disc on the machine, but I have never found that this makes any difference.

Right: Making a pintucked piping to insert in a seam.

Bobbin thread
Use a machine embroidery thread.

Tension
Both the top and bottom tensions should be tighter than usual. The bobbin thread will zigzag between the two top threads, and this zigzag should not be as wide as the tuck. The top threads should barely go through the fabric, so keep altering both tensions until you achieve this.

Foot
It makes your life much easier if you buy a pintuck foot. These come with 9, 7, 5 or 3 grooves. The 9-groove foot is used with the narrowest needle and the finest fabric. The 3-groove foot is used with the needle set to the widest spacing for working on thick fabrics.

Teeth
These should be up.

Stitch
Use a straight stitch.

Stitch length
Normal.

1 Stitch the tucks on the straight grain of the fabric. Place the tuck under the next groove along and stitch the second tuck. The groove will keep the previously stitched tuck parallel to the second one you are doing now. The spaces between the tucks is determined by which groove the previous tucks fit into, and any groove can be used to vary the spacing.

2 When you have finished the pintucking, cut the fabric, on the bias, into strips about 3 cm (1¼ in) wide (according to the size of the piping cord you are using). Fold it around the cord and insert it into the seam as usual, using a piping foot.

Left: Patterned fabric, pintucked, with slashed, burnt and painted folds.

Below left: Fabric made from tiny pieces of plain and patterned fabric was pintucked to secure the tiny pieces and add texture.

Below: Fabric made from layers of chiffon enclosing scraps of gold leaf was pintucked and inserted into a black velvet seam.

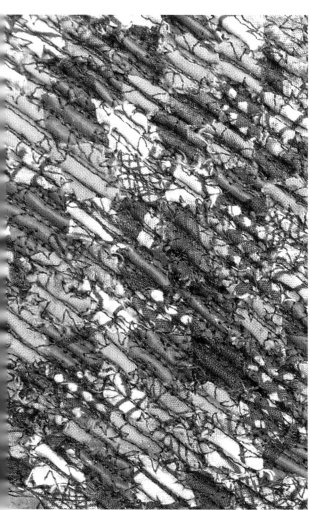

2 STITCHED EDGES

There are many ways of stitching an edge decoratively: a simple satin stitch edging, a corded or wired edge, lacy edges stitched on water-soluble fabric and sewn onto to the embroidery after it has been dissolved, or beaded edges. The last is the only hand technique included in this book, but beads make a wonderful edge to a piece of machine embroidery, adding colour and shine.

Opposite: Bustier with piped seams, lacy edges worked on water-soluble fabric and ruffles edged with automatic stitch patterns. (Elli Woodsford)

Whatever your choice of edge, it must be thought through at the design stage, and must develop from the sort of decoration that has been used on the main piece. Do try some samples, exploring every avenue, trying different techniques to see which one is the most suitable. Think about what you want the edge to do: should it emphasise the colour, add extra shapes in the way of points or tabs, or be fairly neutral so that it does not distract from the main centre of interest?

Sometimes the edge is the only decoration, and the whole piece is composed of multiple edges, perhaps made up of narrow strips, each one with a decorative edge. Also consider the seams. They could be on the outside of the piece, stitched after the edging has been worked.

A tailored edge might be right for a cushion, but an extravagant lacy edge is just what you want on the pages of an 'Elizabethan' style book, or on a bag. Tabs would look good on a cushion or bag, but could be a dreadful nuisance on something else.

Right: An edge stitched with a larger automatic pattern. This is an official edging pattern.

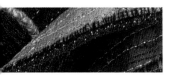

Satin stitch edges

Satin stitch, or a close zigzag stitch, gives a wonderful finish to an edge, whether it is on an applied shape or a freestanding piece of embroidery. Use a thread in a different colour from the main fabric or stitching to give a clear, clean line, emphasising the shape. Straight lines or gentle curves are the easiest to do – it's probably best to steer clear of complicated shapes, treating them in another way.

When applying one piece of a fabric to another, back it with Bondaweb and then iron it onto the background fabric. This will hold it in place while you stitch it.

Method

Fabrics
Choose fairly firm, closely woven fabrics. Velvets, scrim, very stretchy fabrics, or textured or lacy fabrics are better treated using another method.

Frame
Use a stabiliser if you need to rather than putting the fabric in a frame. Try a nappy-liner, or tissue paper, or if these are too soft, use one of the commercial stabilisers.

Needle
Try a 90 unless you are using very delicate fabrics.

Top thread
Machine embroidery thread.

Bobbin thread
Any thread can be used, as it will not affect the surface.

Tension
Use a slightly loose top tension so that the bobbin thread does not show.

Foot
Appliqué foot.

Teeth
These should be up.

Stitch
Use a zigzag stitch set at nearly 0. Try this on samples first to get the length right.

1 Stitch slowly and evenly, working from one corner to the next. Then lift the foot, rotate the fabric and work along the second edge.

2 Lettuce edges are created by working on the folded edge of a very stretchy fabric. Start stitching at the beginning of the fold, and then pull the fabric hard as you stitch to give the wavy edge.

To cover a corner, zigzag right to the edge, then turn the fabric and work the second size from the edge.

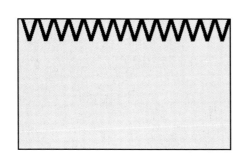

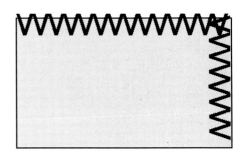

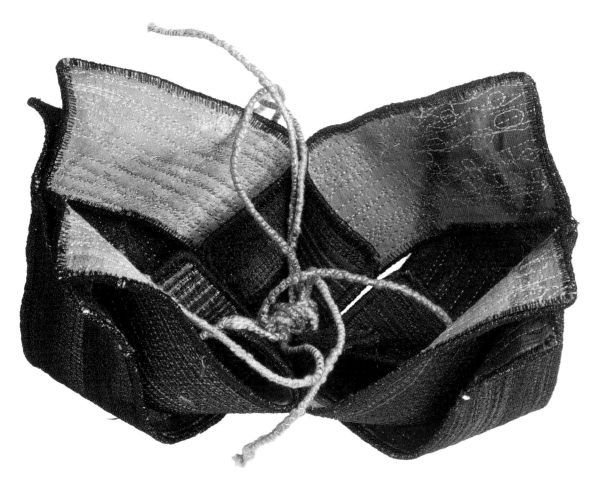

Left: Vessel with satin-stitched edges on embroidered wired pieces, with a zigzag cord imitating stamens of a flower.

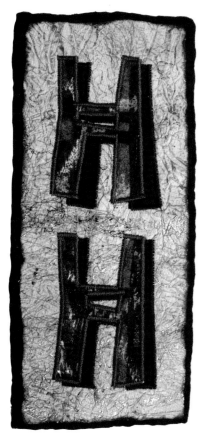

Far left: Hard-edged appliqué using satin stitch.

Left: Lettuce edges worked on a very stretchy fabric.

Corded edges

A satin stitch edge is not always the answer, and little tufts of the fabric can show, or the edge may be uneven. Enclosing a cord in the stitching will solve the problem, especially on firmer pieces of embroidery. You can use leather thonging, gimp, string, a twisted cord, a thick linen thread, or anything else you can find that is firm enough.

Keep to simple shapes and plan how to treat the corners. The cord you are covering can follow the corner closely, or if it is a decorative one, the cord can be looped at the corner, knotted or left hanging freely – it all depends on the character of the piece you are edging.

Method

Fabrics
These must be firm – you cannot easily stitch a corded edge on a floppy fabric.

Needle
Choose a needle size suitable for the thread you are stitching with.

Top thread
Use a machine embroidery thread, coloured or metallic.

Bobbin thread
On three-dimensional pieces this will show, so use a matching thread.

Tension
Normal.

Foot
Use the overlock foot if you have one. The little metal rod will lie between the edge of the fabric and the cord, and prevent the fabric from rolling over. If the stitches are too loose using this foot, use the satin stitch foot.

Teeth
These should be up.

Stitch
Work zigzag stitch, fairly close together. Try some samples to find the best width and length. You might want to use an open zigzag so that a decorative cord shows between the stitches.

Stitch the first edge, and, when you come to the corner, take the cord around the corner while you are stitching it. Do not pull this cord at all – in fact I often push it back slightly so that it does not pull the corner out of shape.

Right: Attaching a cord to an edge, and two different ways of treating the corner.

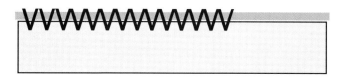

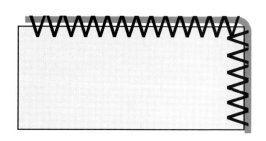

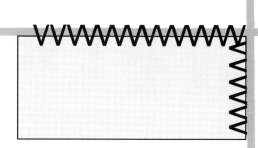

A vessel based on a drawing of a wasps' nest. The edges are finished with leather thong, zigzagged to each piece of embroidery, sandwiched with wire mesh to stiffen it.

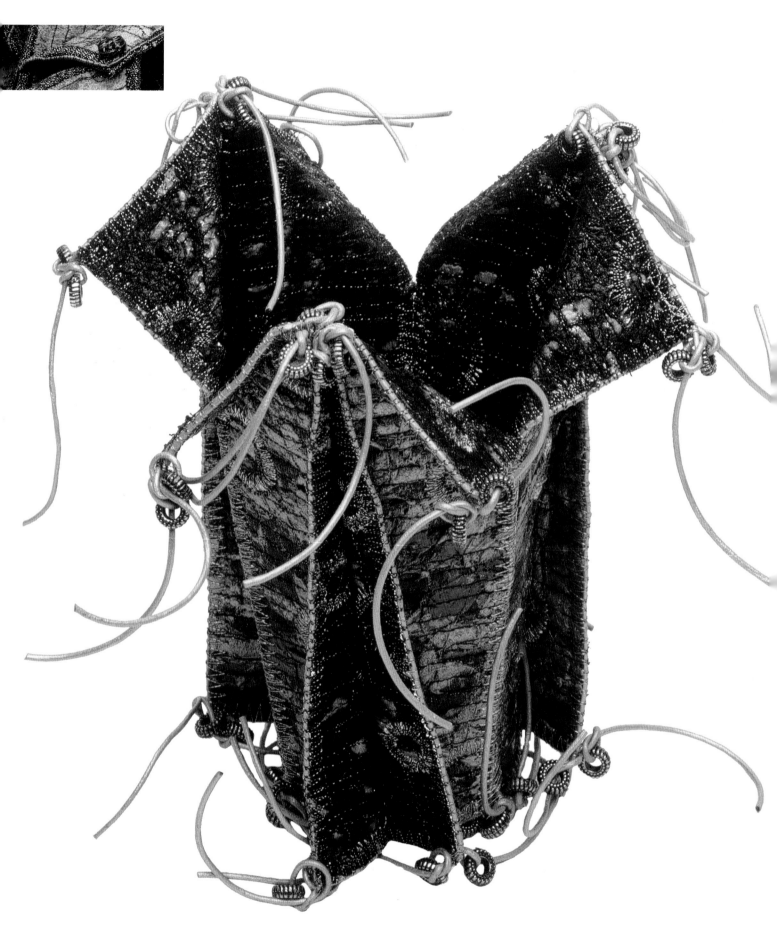

Opposite page: A vessel using stitched paper napkin as a lining, and decorated with Flower Stitcher circles. The edges are finished with metallic cord and knotted at the corners to hold the metal rings.

Left: A vessel made in the same way as above, with each piece of embroidery edged with gimp, secured with rolls of embroidery. (Sue Munday)

Left: The base of the vessel on p. 36, made from three wrapped rings stitched together and painted.

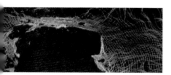

Wired edges

If you wish to make pieces of embroidery that can be coiled, rolled or generally manipulated, it is a good idea to stitch wire around the edge. This can be done on even the finest fabrics, or on machine-made lacy pieces, or thick, heavier embroidery.

Method

Fabrics
Any fabrics that can be placed in a frame are suitable.

Frame
Using a frame is a good idea when you are wiring the edge of a shape such as a leaf or petal.

Needle
Use a size to suit the fabric. For example, do not use too large a needle if it is going to make holes in a delicate fabric.

Top thread
Use machine embroidery thread, either coloured or metallic.

Bobbin thread
If you are using a metallic thread it is not a good idea to use the same thread on the bobbin – a coloured one is better. Remember that it will show, and choose a colour accordingly.

Tension
Normal, or loose (try $2\frac{1}{2}$) if you are using a metallic thread.

Foot
None, or use the free embroidery foot.

Teeth
These should be dropped.

Stitch
Satin stitch or zigzag. Test the width over the wire on a spare piece of fabric.

1 Use wire that is fine enough to bend easily, but thick enough to hold a shape. I use 20- or 24-gauge coloured copper wire as it looks attractive even if the stitches do not completely cover it.

2 Mark the design on the fabric.

3 Make a tiny bend in the end of the wire, and hook it through the fabric at the beginning of the line you wish to stitch, to stop the wire from pulling along. Then stitch over the wire along the design line.

4 When you get near the end of the line, make another hook in the wire and push it through the fabric. Finish the stitching. Flatten the wire hooks.

5 Remove the fabric from the frame, cut around the edge of the stitching, and melt it to neaten the edge. Alternatively, you could run a thread of glue around the edge so that the fabric will never fray.

An edge of wired, painted pipe cleaner, with knotted stuffed knitting ribbon and beads on a distressed chiffon-covered fabric. (Maggie Grey)

A delicate tassel made from wire edged organza shapes, stiffened by a filling of water-soluble fabric. (Penny Usher)

Above: Fuschia tassel with organza petals and wire-stiffened leaf. The stamens are satin stitched string. (Christine Chinn)

Far left: Squashed Fairy tassel with wire-edged organza shapes, stiffened lacy shapes stitched on water-soluble fabric. It is also edged with wire, and Flower Stitcher circles, folded to make small buds. (Sandra Coleridge)

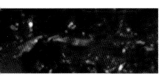

Lacy edges

Stitched patterns and borders on water-soluble fabric can be dissolved and then sewn onto the edge of an embroidery. If you lay the embroidery on water-soluble fabric and then stitch an edge on it, the embroidery often puckers as the lacy edging shrinks, so I always stitch the edging separately and sew it on afterwards.

When you are stitching on any water-soluble fabric, the stitches must link together – otherwise the whole piece falls apart when it has been dissolved. This is really crucial.

Method

FOR FREE EMBROIDERY

Fabrics
Use any cold water-soluble fabric. Draw or trace the pattern onto it using a felt pen of a similar colour to the thread you will use. Very fine water-soluble fabric is difficult to use and can split during stitching, so look for a thicker one.

Frame
If the fabric is thin you will need to use a frame, but if it is thick, or you are using two layers together, you should not need one.

Needle
Use a size to suit the thread. If you are using a metallic thread you will need a size 100 needle, otherwise an 80 or 90 will do.

Top thread
Use a machine embroidery thread, coloured or metallic.

Bobbin thread
This will show, so use a thread that goes with the top thread. Try using a variegated thread on the bobbin with a metallic thread through the needle.

Tension
Normal, or slightly looser for a metallic thread.

Foot
Use a free embroidery or quilting foot.

Teeth
These should be dropped.

Stitch
Start with free running stitch and outline the whole design, going over each line a number of times to link the stitches together. Zigzag can be used over the top to thicken up some of the stitching. If the embroidery is thick enough you can work decorative stitches on top.

FOR AUTOMATIC PATTERNS

When using automatic patterns to make lacy borders, have the satin stitch foot on and leave the teeth up. Work lines of straight stitching and then automatic patterns over the top, overlapping the bands of pattern slightly. You will need to stitch at least five overlapping rows to make a good edge.

To dissolve the fabric, use hot water even though it is called cold water-soluble. Leave the piece to soak and then massage away the gummy residue. Rinse it in clean water.

Another method of dissolving the stitching, if you want to keep the shape as it was when you finished the stitching, is to pin it onto a polystyrene board and then hold it under a hot tap. This takes longer to dissolve, but you can rub it gently with your fingers to help it along.

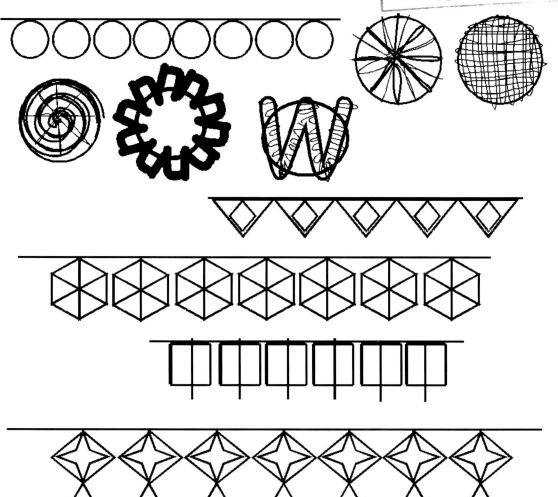

Left: An automatic pattern, stitched in the same direction (top) and in reverse, built up in layers on water-soluble fabric.

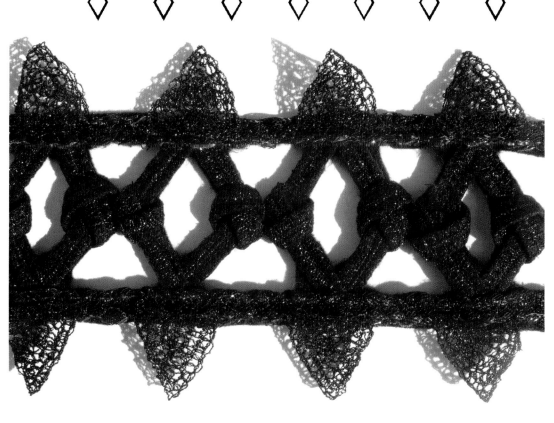

Left: Narrow strips of firm felt are zigzagged over and knotted. They are held together with a stitched thread braid and decorated with lacy triangles worked on water-soluble fabric.

Right top: Drawing of a patterned edging on paper.

Right centre: The pattern traced onto cold-water-soluble fabric and the stitching begun.

Right bottom: The finished stitching pinned to the board after dissolving the fabric.

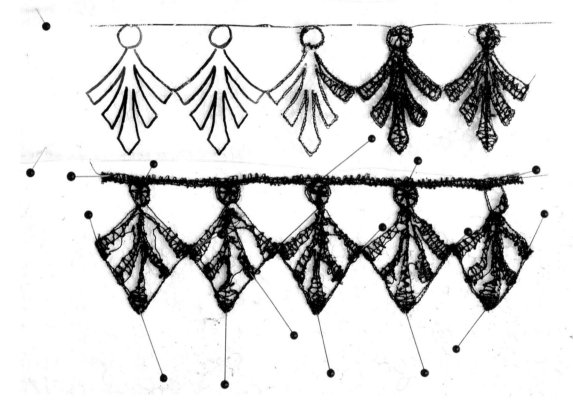

Below: Designs for similar edges.

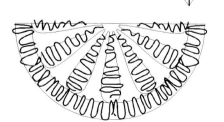

Far left: Sample of a piece of machine embroidery edged with machine-made lace

Left: Samples of edges stitched on water-soluble fabric with the same stitching after the fabric has been dissolved.

Left: A computer design for embroidery with similar machine-made lacy edging.

Below: A panel of distressed paper and fabric with stitched, cut out and burnt spiral shapes, and a machine-made lacy edging.

Opposite: A panel of distressed paper and fabric with a top layer of a grid, satin stitched on water-soluble fabric and torn into scraps, edges with firmly stitched discs.

Buttonhole edges

Most machines will do automatic, or at least semi-automatic, buttonholes, which takes the angst out of doing a large number of them. On computerised machines you can type in the length that you want and everything is set for you – you can just stitch buttonholes for ever.

Mark the top of the buttonholes on the fabric using a fabric marker or a coloured pencil. Take note of where this mark shows against the buttonhole foot so that you start in the same place every time, and do not work too near the edge.

Method

Fabrics
You can work a buttonhole on almost any fabric, but use a stabiliser if the fabric is very fine or floppy.

Frame
No frame is needed.

Needle
Find one to suit the thread. Use a size 100 if you are using a metallic thread.

Top thread
Use any machine embroidery thread, coloured or metallic.

Bobbin thread
Use a machine embroidery thread.

Tension
Normal.

Foot
Use the automatic buttonhole foot.

Teeth
These should be up.

Stitch
Your machine will automatically use the correct width of satin stitch.

Stitch length
This will also be set by the machine.

Decorative buttonholes can have braids or cords woven through them, be folded in half to make tabs, or cut out of the fabric and sewn back onto some embroidery. Buttonholes worked on water-soluble fabric, over the top of some previously sewn patterns, add richness and strength to a lacy border.

Buttonholes, worked on felt, were cut around to make tabs, and the border decorated with couching, and cinq point de venise loops.

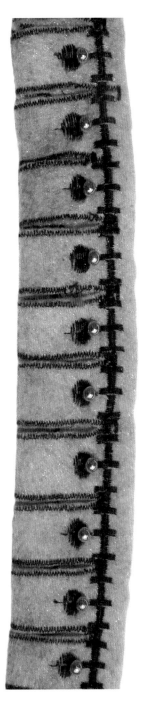

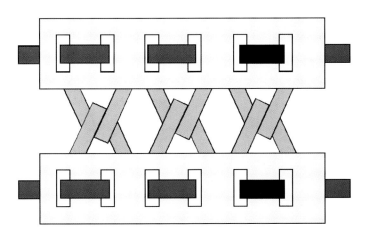

Left: Design for an edge with buttonholes and twisted rouleaux.

Far left: Extra long buttonholes worked on felt, cut and folded to make tabs.

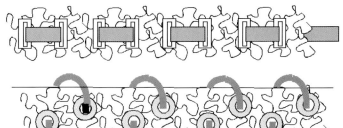

Left: Designs for buttonholes worked on automatic stitched patterns, threaded with ribbons.

Left: Sample of patterned stitching on water-soluble fabric, then being dissolved and threaded with zigzagged cord.

Far left: Buttonholes, cut and stitched to make a raised surface. (Maggie Grey)

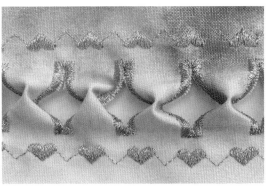

Left: Prairie Points and buttonholes, cut and stitched to make a raised surface and threaded with cord. (Maggie Grey)

Patterned edges

The automatic patterns make a very pretty edging and take the hassle out of stitching repeat patterns freehand. Sometimes the edge needs to be stabilised first with a couple of lines of straight stitching, or you can even use a previously stitched corded edge, so that it does not stretch when the pattern is stitched. Not all patterns are suitable for this, so try some of them on a spare bit of fabric first. A satin stitch pattern is the best and those with a straight line on one side of the pattern are the most useful, and conceal the edge better.

Method

Fabrics
A firm fabric is the best, or use a stabiliser.

Frame
This is not necessary.

Needle
Use a size to suit the thread. If you are using a metallic thread, use a size 100 needle.

Top thread
Use a machine embroidery thread, coloured or metallic.

Bobbin thread
This will show, so it should match the top thread. If you have trouble using a metallic thread on the bobbin as well as the top, change it for a coloured thread.

Tension
Slightly loose.

Foot
Use the satin stitch foot.

Teeth
These should be up.

Stitch
Use an automatic pattern stitch.

Stitch length
The machine will set this for your particular selection of stitch.

An alternative way of using these patterns is to stitch them on a straight strip of fabric, then cut them out and stitch them to an edge. Use short lengths as flaps, or to make a border near an edge. A good fabric to use for this is felt, as it is easy to cut, and the edges can always be singed if you want them to be very close to the stitching.

a

b

Above: Automatic patterns stitched on an edge or fold of fabric.

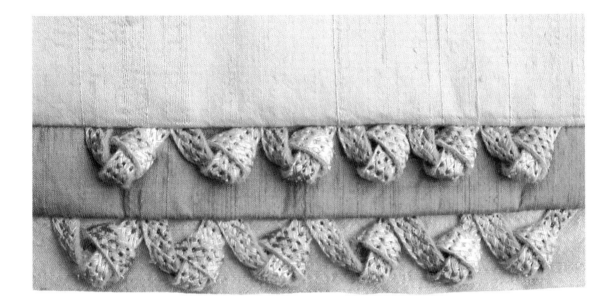

Left: Automatic patterns, worked in strips and cut out, knotted and inserted into a seam. (Lynn Horniblow)

Below: A fringe with a heading and dangles using automatic patterns. (Lynn Horniblow)

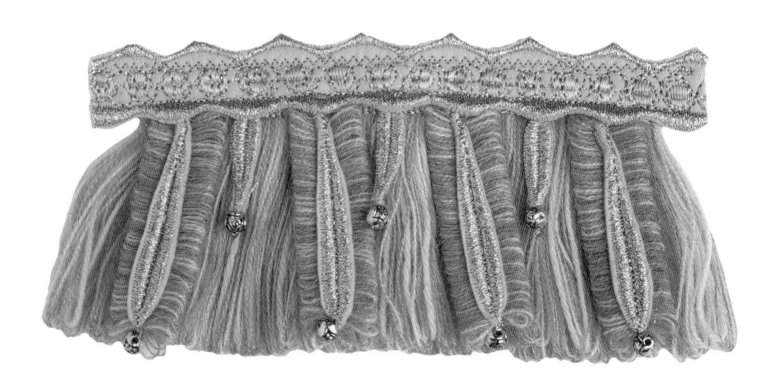

Wild Tassel with petals made with organza and machine made lace, edged with an automatic pattern. (Tracey Cooke)

Bag of ruffles
made of
transparent fabrics,
edged with an
automatic pattern,
cut out with a
soldering iron.
(Elli Woodsford)

Embroidered slips on edges

Opposite: Vessel made from paper beads, wrapped with stitched slips. The base is similar to the piece on p. 54.

Pieces of embroidery, also known as slips or patches, can be stitched to an edge to make an interesting border. These can be embroidered freehand, or designed in the sewing machine software. They must be reasonably stiff with a lot of stitching, and can be used flat on the edge or folded over it.

It is usually better to stitch them onto the edge using freehand straight stitch, as invisibly as possible, using a thread that matches the background colour. The texture can be built up using scraps of fabrics, small pieces of knotted cord, small cut-up pieces of other embroideries, or stitched papers.

The edge of the embroidery should be finished off in some way before the slips are attached. It can be melted, hemmed or backed with another fabric, and seamed as if you were making an edging on a garment.

Above: Two possibilities for edges decorated with large embroidered shapes.

Right: Three separately embroidered pieces, or slips, decorating the edges of a richly stitched triangle.

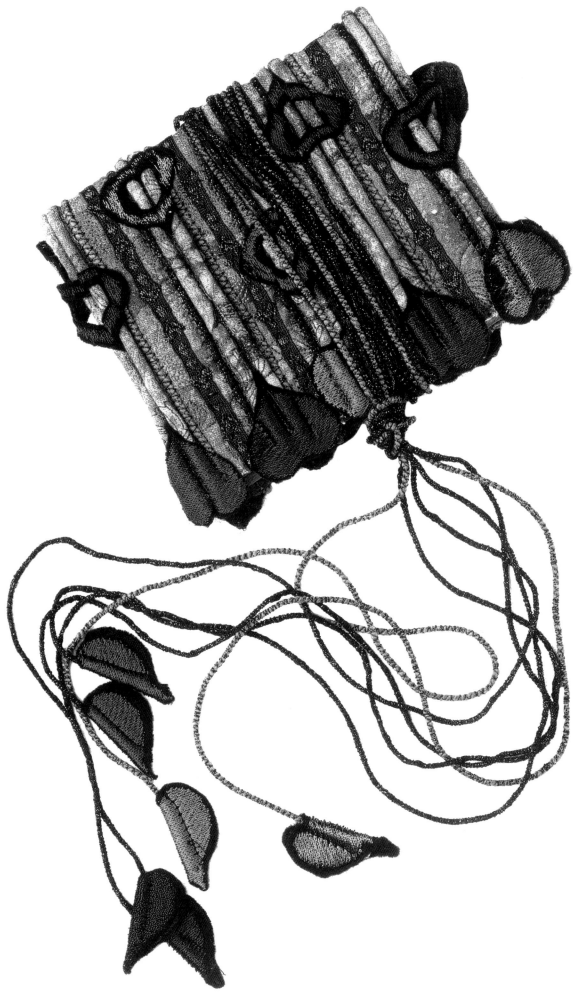

Opposite: A computer design of distorted knots was stitched and applied to the edge of the stripped fabric.

Right: Hearts were stitched separately and attached to the edges of this book cover.

Beaded edges

Opposite: Three tassels with beaded edge: left, a pattern on a Bernina sewing machine card was cut out and the edges burnt and beaded; centre, a tassel using the ruffs and balls described on p. 58; right, part of pattern on a Pfaff sewing machine card was cut out and beaded. Two of these were sewn together to make a three dimensional shape at the top, and two more for the bottom one.

The simplest beaded edge seems to be the most effective, as complex ones sometimes take over, with their character dominating the whole piece of embroidery. Beads add colour and glisten and provide the opportunity to do a little hand stitching – a nice change after the machining. They also give some protection to a stitched edge.

The beads can be tiny on small items, or quite big and decorative on larger ones, and include decorated paper beads that you have made yourself.

A little space between the beads always looks better than when they are sewn in a solid line.

Method

Fabrics
The edge on which you are going to sew the beads can be satin stitched, burnt, wired or just folded fabric. There must be a little body to stitch onto, so a single layer of fabric is usually not enough, so do a trial piece first.

Needle
Use a size 10 beading needle for most small beads, or a sewing needle for slightly larger beads.

Thread
Use a beading thread if the beads are tiny, or an ordinary sewing thread if they are bigger. Choose a colour that is similar to the colour of the fabric so that the stitches do not show.

Right: Threaded circles, beaded and pulled up to make a ball.

For a single-beaded edge, start with a few back stitches to anchor the thread, then thread one bead onto the needle and stitch through the fabric. Take another stitch through the fabric, thread another bead on, and go through the fabric again. For a three-beaded edge, pick up three beads on each alternate stitch.

Beaded ruffs and balls
On the tassel head shown here, ten stitched rings were beaded on the edge, and then threaded onto a thick sewing thread which was pulled up tight and tied in a knot to hold the ruff before being sewed to the neck of a previously made tassel.

On the hanging braids, four rings were also threaded and pulled up tight around the zigzagged cord to make a ball.

a

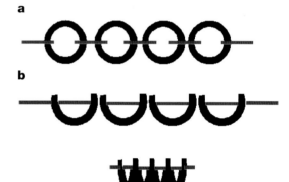

b

Above: a) Tiny beads sewn to an edge. b) Flower Stitched circles were threaded onto a fine cord and pulled up to make ruffles and balls.

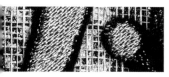

Larger beads

For larger embroideries, and when beaded edges on a larger scale are needed, you can either buy large commercial beads or, more fun, make your own. Beads can be made from a number of different things, but I like making a cylindrical paper base and then wrapping things around them. What you wrap the cylinders with can totally alter the look of the bead and can be wire, strips of painted nappy-liner or wisps of tri-lobal nylon melted with a heat gun, narrow strips of twisted polythene bags also melted with a heat gun, glue or

Homemade beads made using rolled paper, decorated with metallic threads, wire, nappy liners, scraps of Angelina and tri-lobal nylon. Some of these were carved using a soldering iron, some melted with heat gun, and many others were painted.

melted sealing wax dribbled around the bead, or more paper strips to give a sculptured look.

The beads in the embroidery on the opposite page were attached to the work with short lengths of ribbon, but every type of bead will demand a different method. If they are irregular or wired, then you can sew through the gaps or through the wires. Some beads will need to be attached by sewing through the centre hole, in which case make sure that they are fairly short or they will sag.

Method

1 Cut a strip of paper about 20 cm (8 in) long, and from 1 to 5 cm (½ to 2 in) wide. If it is wider than this, it is difficult to roll up.

2 Dribble a strip of glue down the centre of the strip to within about 1 cm (½ in) from one end. If you use the thick tacky PVA, it does not matter if it gets onto the front of the bead because you will paint it afterwards.

3 Starting from this end, roll the paper tightly around a kebab stick or double-ended knitting needle. Do this on a table and press down hard as you roll, to keep the bead tight.

4 When you come to the end, spread a little more glue across the end and press it firmly onto the bead.

5 Leave it to dry for several hours.

6 If you wish to then decorate the bead with more strips of paper, or use any of the above suggestions, do it now. Then paint the bead with acrylic paint, either coloured or metallic.

Further decoration in the form of waxes or embossing powders can be a final flourish.

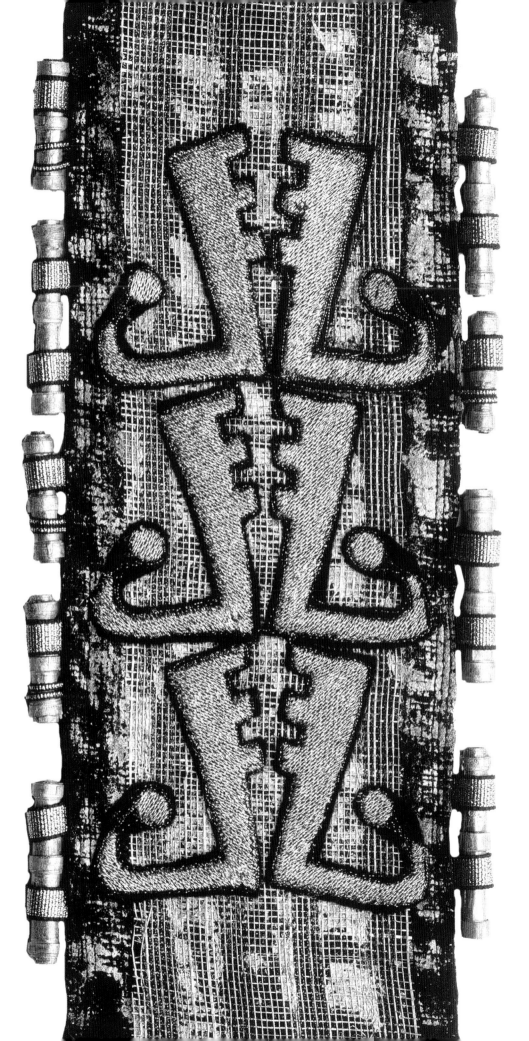

Complex paper beads were attached to an edge with metallic ribbons.

Joining edges

Opposite: Different ways of stitching to join or disguise edges of embroidery.

You may wish to join edges to make a wider braid or even a whole fabric. Try strips of braid, cords, pieces of fabric, stitched motifs or cut-up pieces of stitching. The edges can be nearly touching or with space between them to give a more delicate effect. The stitching secures the edges and blends them into each other. We are used to doing this as a hand-stitching technique using insertion stitches, but using either the automatic patterns on a sewing machine, or free machine embroidery, across the space will do the same job with a different look.

There are many ways of doing this but probably the easiest is to lay the strips or other shapes on a heavy water-soluble fabric or water-soluble paper and then lightly stitch the pieces to hold them in place while you work over the edges and across the space. You can build up the effect by laying strips of organza, net, ribbons or scraps of other fabrics in the space, holding them with pins and then simply stitching them together before working the decorative stitching.

Right: Frayed edged fabric shapes and scraps of embroidery were laid on water-soluble fabric and joined with free machine embroidery before dissolving.

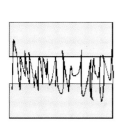 

Wavy scribble – free running or whip stitch. Make sure the stitches interlock.

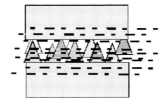

Cable stitch over tiny piece of fabric.

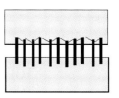

Satin stitch bars – good on water-soluble fabric. Cords or narrow braids can be woven through.

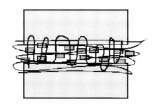

A grid of free running or whip stitch, with satin stitch blobs or 'beads'.

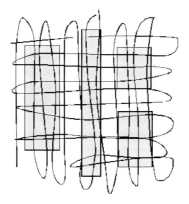

Grid over applied shapes or on water-soluble fabric.

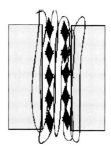

Automatic patterns partly covered and disrupted with free running stitch worked on top of them.

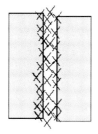

Swinging stitches – an automatic pattern worked while moving the fabric from side to side.

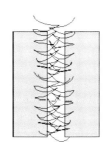

Meandering – free running or whip stitch. Try different movements, small circles or vermicelli.

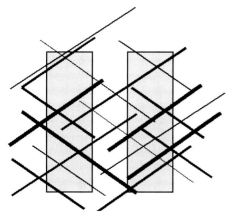

Short lengths of cord or thick threads, zigzagged down

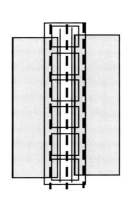

Stitched 'braid' on water-soluble fabric applied over the edges and stitched over the top

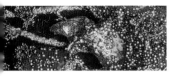

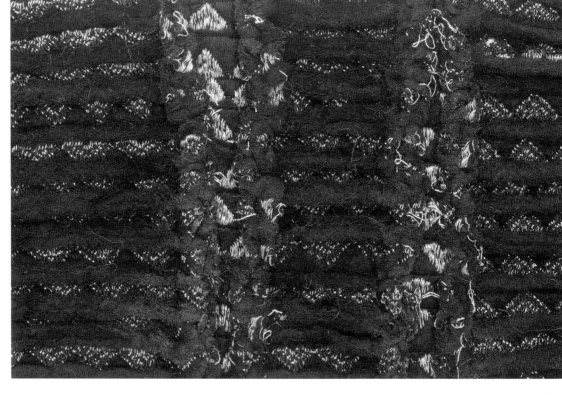

Right: Seams can be on the right side to add texture.

Below: A complex piece of drawn thread embroidery was edged with decorated fabric strips. (Gill Morgan)

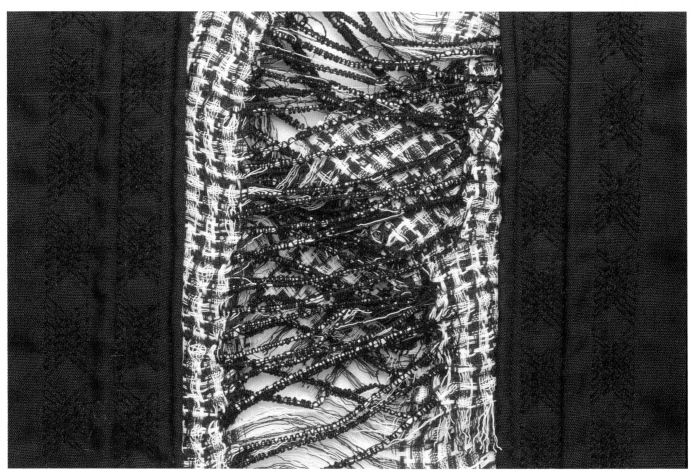

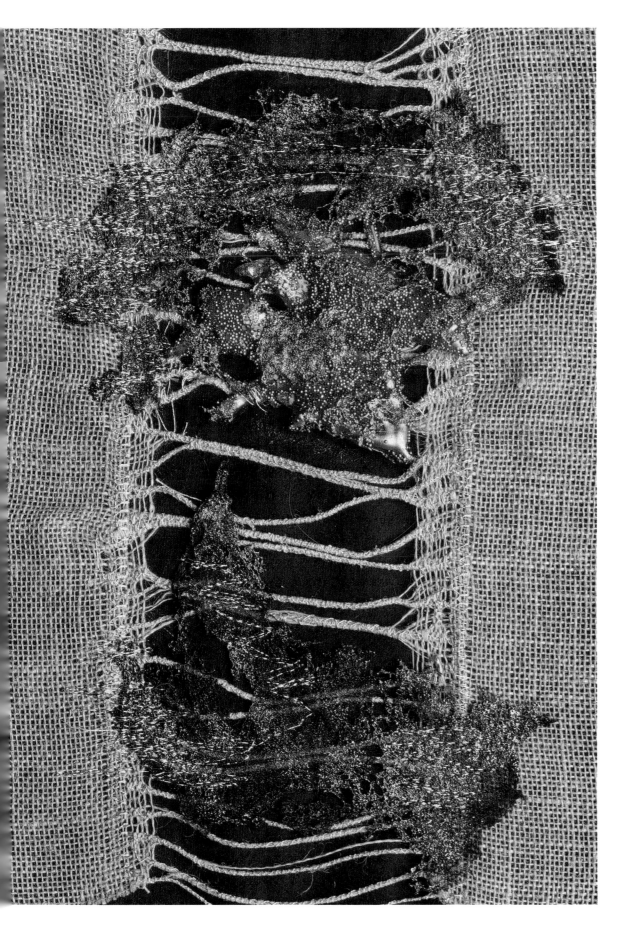

Drawn thread embroidery, machine-stitched on scrim, was edged with zigzag to prevent further movement of the threads. It was decorated with stitching and paint on chiffon, melted glue gun shapes with paint, wisps of chiffon, paint and tiny gold balls. Free running attached the pieces to the scrim. (Jacqui Brimacomb)

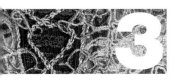

3 FRINGES

Often a fringe is just the thing to use on the edges of a small bag, around a tassel, a lampshade, a cushion, a sleeve, or a wall hanging. The design must be based on the design of the object it is to decorate, using the same colours, the same threads if possible, and maybe the same type of stitching. If you do not have yarn of the right colour, then you can dye it first or paint it on the frame. Printing and stencilling a pattern on a wrapped fringe can tie it in with the same printing or stencilling on the embroidery that the fringe is attached to.

The proportion is crucial – not only the length of the fringe, but what it is made of. A fringe made using a zigzag cord will be chunkier than one stitched on water-soluble fabric. Try using the Fibonacci series of numbers to gauge the depth of the fringe. These are 1, 2, 3, 5, 8, 13 and 21, and can be calculated using centimetres or inches. You will not really need to go any higher than this. For example, if your bag measures 20 cm from top to bottom, the fringe could be 7.5, 12.5 or 20 cm deep and any of these would look right – or use a tiny 2.5 cm fringe, almost a ruff, right round the edge. (Using imperial measurements: on a bag measuring 8 inches, the fringe could be 3, 5 or 8 inches deep, or even 1 inch.)

Look for a yarn that behaves in the way you want it to on your fringe. Woollen yarn will be bouncy, a zigzagged cord will be stiff and formal, a rayon weaving yarn will hang beautifully, and strips of fabric can be twisted and informal, or made of organza to give a delicate look. Beads can be incorporated, either bought or home-made, as can really crazy things such as wood shavings or bamboo sticks, painted to tie in with the main piece.

The fringe can be cut or left in loops, and you can hang all sorts of things from the loops, such as rings, tassels or beads. These must be threaded onto the yarn before it is wrapped around the frame, and left hanging at one edge, stitching it at the other.

A delicate fringe stitched on water-soluble fabric can be embroidered separately and stitched on afterwards. If you lay the fabric on the water-soluble fabric and then stitch the fringe through both layers, the fabric tends to cockle. It seems better to stitch the fringe, then, before dissolving it, apply it to a braid stitched on water-soluble fabric and the whole thing dissolved together. Or dissolve the stitched fringe and then apply it to the fabric edge after it has dried. It is easier to gauge the length properly and some can be cut off the length, or more added, if necessary.

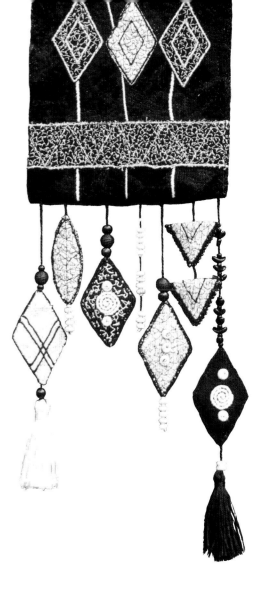

The embroidered and stuffed shapes in the fringe echo the shapes on the main part of the panel. Beads and tassels add variety. (Ruby Lever)

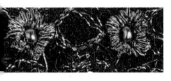

Delicate flower fringe

This fringe is worked using the Flower Stitcher attachment, combined with free stitchery, on water-soluble fabric. You can also design these rings or flowers on the sewing machine software. They would look lovely around the skirt of a tassel, or on the bottom of a bag or lampshade.

The stitching can be done on one layer of the fabric but it is actually much easier to work a number of flowers, then the braid, then cut them all out roughly, and put them back onto a new piece of water-soluble fabric, building up the fringe as you want it to look. When there are as many layers to dissolve as this, even using hot water it can take at least half an hour, but it is a more flexible method.

Method

Fabrics
Use heavyweight water-soluble fabric, or two layers of a finer one, so that you do not have to use an embroidery frame.

Attachment
The Flower Stitcher – this will fit most low-shank machines (for Berninas you need a standard adapter). It will not fit some other machines so you will need to try it. Fit it onto your machine according to the instruction leaflet that comes with the attachment.

One word of warning: after a while, the attachment will seize up and not move at all. Just put a tiny drop of oil wherever metal touches metal, and you will have no more trouble for years.

Needle
Use a size to fit the thread.

Top thread
Any machine embroidery thread, coloured or metallic, can be used.

Bobbin thread
Use any thread, but it will show, so choose carefully. You might like to use a different colour on the bobbin.

Tension
Normal, both top and bottom.

Presser foot pressure
Set this to the maximum.

Teeth
Drop the teeth.

Stitch
Use a utility stitch, or an open, simple pattern.

Try some of the patterns on a spare bit of fabric to find the prettiest, but do not use any with satin stitching as the close stitching will tear the fabric.

1 To make a large flower, set the Flower Stitcher to the + sign, and move your needle as far to the right as it will go.

2 Place the fabric under the rubber ring and just press the foot pedal. Make sure the fabric can rotate without getting caught up in anything.

3 Work a number of these flowers all over the fabric, and then work some smaller ones moving the Flower Stitcher to the – sign.

4 When you have finished, cut the flowers out roughly.

Different sized rings to be worked on the Flower Stitcher for the fringe.

Above: A fringe worked using the Flower Stitcher on sold water-soluble fabric, with extra rings and beads adding richness to the edge.

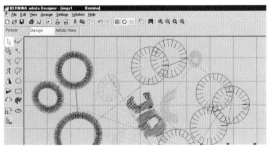

Far left: If you have any of the sewing machine computer programs you can design and stitch these rings on it.

Left: The Flower Stitcher attachment. It will fit most sewing machines.

The hanging 'strings'

Lay the rings on a new piece of water-soluble fabric and work free machining over them, round and round the circle to hold the stitches together, perhaps a spider's web across them, and then in a line down the middle, using three or four rows of stitching to hold the rings in place. Then cut these 'strings' out roughly.

The braid

Using the same utility or pattern stitch, on water-soluble fabric, work overlapping bands the length you wish the fringe to be. Use a large piece of fabric so that you can add the 'strings' to the braid.

Then work lots of rows of straight stitching over the top to hold the patterned stitching in place, at least nine or ten rows on 1 cm (1/2 in) braid.

Putting it all together

Pin the strings to the braid so that the top circles just overlap the bottom edge of the braid. Secure them with a line of free machining. You might wish to add another layer of strings on top, and then stitch them on too.

Decorating the fringe

You can add more rings onto the braid, using free machining, and also more rings on top of the hanging rings if you wish. Work these tiny rings on net with the Flower Stitcher set to the – sign, the needle as far left as it will go, and satin stitch at width 5. Then cut them out close to the stitching.

Dissolving the fringe

Use warm or hot water, even though the instructions usually say cold, and leave the whole thing until the fabric has completely dissolved. Dab it with a kitchen paper towel to remove most of the moisture, and leave it to dry on a plastic bag. You might like to spread the rings out at this stage, or you can leave them curled.

Added decoration

Small rings, worked on net, can be stitched onto the fringe, and beads sewn on by hand.

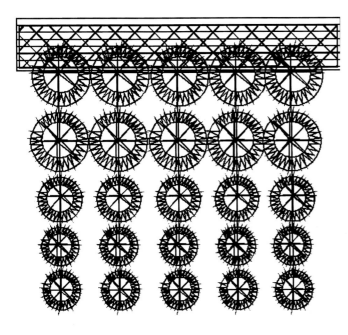

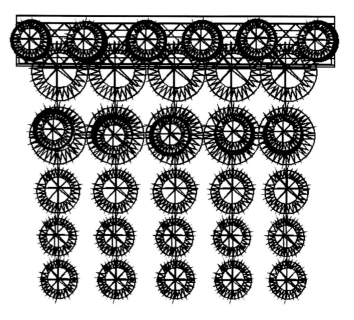

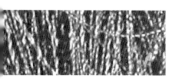

Satin stitch rings

*Opposite top:
Braid made with
plaited strips of
embroidery, and
four leaf clovers
made from satin
stitched rings,
folded over a
central ring to
give body.
(Lynn Horniblow)*

This is a chunkier fringe also made using the Flower Stitcher. If you do not have one of these attachments you can make extra large eyelets using the eyelet attachment, which gives a similar result. These sturdier rings can be folded and twisted in many ways to give different effects, so when you have made a number of them, cut them out and sit and play with them to see what you can do.

Method

Fabrics

Use two layers of felt. Do not use too large a piece as it needs to rotate easily while stitching.

*Opposite below:
Similar stitched
and folded rings to
make a heading for
a fringe.*

Needle

Use a size to suit the thread.

Top thread

Use a machine embroidery thread, coloured or metallic.

Bobbin thread

A coloured thread is best, unless you will see both sides of the ring and need to match a metallic thread that you are using through the needle.

Tension

Normal top tension, or slightly loose for a metallic thread. Normal bobbin tension.

Attachment

Fit the Flower Stitcher onto your sewing machine according to the instructions. It will fit most machines, but you may need an adapter if yours is a low-shank sewing machine. Alternatively, you can design these in your sewing machine software if you have it. Some machines have good eyelet attachments which will allow you to make very large eyelets, or you could work them freehand over a circle drawn on the fabric, but this takes practice to do well.

Presser foot pressure

If you can adjust this on your machine, set it at maximum pressure.

Teeth

Drop the teeth.

Stitch

Use a zigzag stitch at width 5.

1 To make the largest possible ring, move the Flower Stitcher so that the tongue points to the + sign, and move your needle as far to the right as your machine will allow.

2 Place the double layer of felt under the Flower Stitcher and lower the presser foot lever.

3 Stitch around the ring three times, each one on top of another, to make it richer. Finish with two or three straight stitches to secure the thread. Work a number of these rings.

For maximum stiffness

Cut out the centres only of all the rings, close to the stitching, and singe them with a nightlight. Then cut the rings away from the fabric and singe them on the outside.

For a less stiff result

Cut the rings away from the felt as neatly as you can and do not singe the edges.

For an even softer result

Use only one layer of felt.

Decorating the edges

A beaded edge looks good on these rings, or you can work a hand edging stitch.

The whole ring can be zigzagged freehand over the first stitching, using a wider zigzag to cover the cut edge nicely.

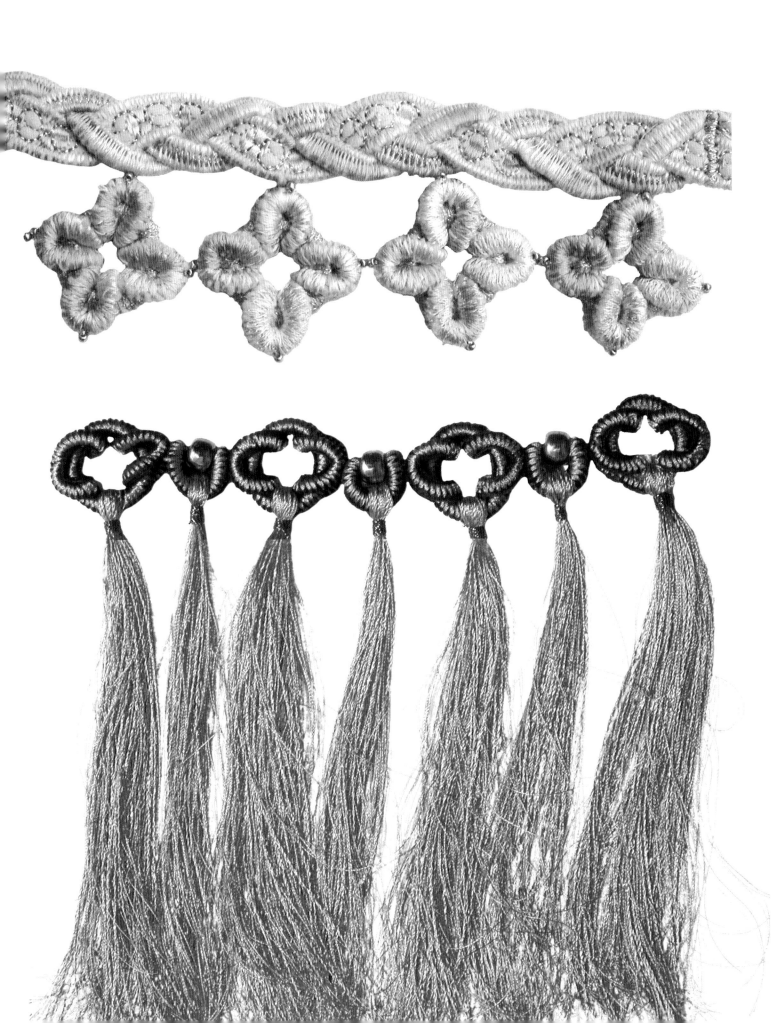

Double-sided fringes or ruffs

These narrow fringes can be used on an edge, to cover a seam, or as surface decoration on a fabric. A braid can be added down the centre, or they can be folded in half to make a double-fringed edge. The edges can be left as loops or can be cut. A narrow fringe can be laid on top of a wider one, or short lengths can be used to decorate other fringes.

As the fringe comes off the frame it will corkscrew, but don't worry – it will lie perfectly flat when stitched down, or you can take advantage of the corkscrew and use it hanging vertically as another fringe. There is no limit to the length you can make, as you keep sliding the length you have stitched off the frame and then winding more yarn on it to make another length.

Method

Yarns
The fringe can be made from rayon tassel yarns, machine embroidery threads, woollen yarn, silk threads, or a previously zigzagged or handmade cord.

Frame
You will need a hairpin crochet hook, or a narrow fringe frame, or a tassel frame which takes apart, for this method.

Needle
Use a size to fit the sewing thread.

Top thread
Use a machine embroidery thread, coloured or metallic.

Bobbin thread
Use a coloured machine embroidery thread. Do not use a metallic thread on the bobbin as well as through the needle unless you really have to.

Tension
Slightly loose on the top, normal on the bobbin.

Foot
Do not use a foot as the space within the frame is usually too narrow. If you are using a wider frame then you can use a darning or embroidery foot.

Teeth
Drop the teeth.

Stitch
Straight stitch.

1 Leaving the spacer bar on the hairpin hook, tie one end of the yarn or yarns to the open end. This is crucial as you will slide the fringe off this end as you stitch it.

2 Wrap the yarn or yarns closely around the hook nearly to the other end and leave the ends hanging.

3 Place the hook under the sewing machine needle and start stitching near the spacer bar along the centre. Carefully move the hook towards the back of the machine until you have stitched nearly the whole length. Then work three more rows of stitching down the centre, back and forth, to secure the yarns.

4 Remove the spacer bar and slide most of the stitched fringe off the hook, leaving about 2.5 cm (1 in) of fringe still on it. Then replace the spacer bar. Wrap more yarns around the hook and stitch them as before. Make sure you do not stitch over the finished fringe. Keep on going until the fringe is as long as you wish, as it can be cut into shorter lengths afterwards.

Left: A hairpin crochet hook, wrapped with yarn and stitched to make a double-sided fringe.

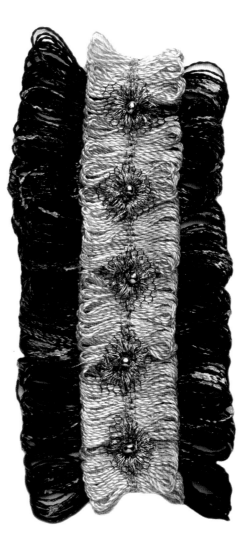

Left: Two double-sided fringes, further decorated with knots, bundles and stitched rings.

Fringes on a frame

This is probably the easiest way to make a fringe, by wrapping threads or yarns around a wire frame and then machine stitching along one edge. The only limit is the length of the fringe, as the frames cannot really be any longer than about 56 cm (22 in), so it could fit the side of a cushion. Build this into your design so that you have joins at the corners, or along one edge only, or make a multiple fringe that is a decorative part of the design.

Method

Yarns
The fringe can be made from rayon tassel yarns, machine embroidery threads, woollen yarn, silk threads, strips of fabric or a previously zigzagged or handmade cord.

Frame
You will need a wire frame that is as long as and slightly deeper than you need the fringe to be. This frame can be made from an old wire coathanger, taped together with parcel tape, or you can buy one (see the Suppliers list on page 126). If you wish to have a looped fringe, then the frame must come apart, so use a hairpin crochet hook or a tassel frame. For a cut fringe it need not come apart.

Needle
Use a size to suit the sewing thread.

Top thread
Use a machine embroidery thread, coloured or metallic.

Bobbin thread
Use a coloured machine embroidery thread. Do not use a metallic thread on the bobbin as well as through the needle unless you really have to.

Tension
Slightly loose on the top, normal on the bobbin.

Foot
Use the piping foot. You can remove the foot altogether if you do not have a piping foot.

Teeth
Leave the teeth up if you are using the piping foot.

Stitch
Use a straight stitch.

Stitch length
Normal.

1 Tie one end of the yarn (multiple yarns if you are using fine threads) onto one edge of the frame. Wrap the yarn or yarns closely around the frame or hook working nearly to the other end. The threads should lie very close together or the fringe will be too thin and weedy. Tie the final end securely on the same side as the first tie. This will be the top of the fringe, the edge you will stitch.

2 Move the needle to one side of the piping foot (if you need to) and stitch near the top edge of the fringe. When you come to the end, turn the frame around and stitch back along the same side. You may need to move the needle so that it stitches on the correct side of the piping foot. Work about four rows of stitching.

3 Steam the fringe thoroughly, using either a flat-bottomed non-electric kettle or a steam iron. Leave the iron propped upright and press the button that produces extra steam. An electric kettle will not do as it keeps cutting out before enough steam emerges to do the job.

4 Either cut the fringe off the frame on both edges, or open the frame and slide the fringe off. This will need some manoeuvring, sliding the fringe partly off one edge to release the tension at the other end of the frame.

When the fringe has been taken off the frame, you can stitch a ribbon or braid to the top edge if this suits your design. If not, lay a fold of the fabric over the top edge to hide the stitching and top-stitch on the fold.

If you are using strips of fabric these can be embroidered, and the edges can be torn or cut with pinking shears. The strips can be cut on the straight or on the bias – you need to experiment with the fabric you are using to see which looks the best. The edges could be narrowly satin stitched.

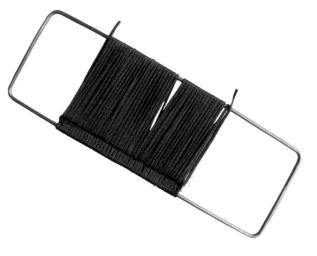

Left: A tassel frame wrapped with yarn.

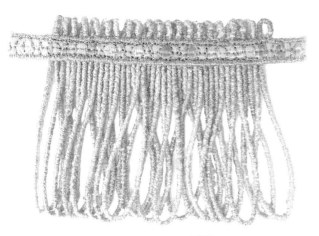

Far left: A fringe made on this frame using zigzag cord and a strip of embroidery as the heading. (Lynn Horniblow)

Left: The frame was wrapped with zigzag cord, threaded with metal rings. Tassels were made on the rings later.

Left: A fringe made by wrapping multi-coloured strips of stitched organza: one on a wider frame and one on a narrower one give different lengths.

Painted fringes

If you do not have the right coloured yarn for a fringe, you can dab a pale-coloured yarn with one or more colours so that it matches or tones with the piece of embroidery it is meant to enhance. It is easier to paint the fringe while it is still on the frame. Dilute silk paints are the best as they do not stiffen the fringe nor make the loops stick together. Using a sponge or a paintbrush, dab the colour onto the yarn, or paint it in strips, on both sides, and leave to dry. You can then heat-set the colour using a hairdryer.

If you wish to use metallic paint, do so, dabbing it on with a brush, and just pull the loops apart from each other when it is dry and you have taken the fringe off the frame.

A fringe made on a hairpin crochet frame, removed from the frame and thickly painted with gold paint, allowing it to twist and turn as it was being painted.

Printing a fringe

You can also print onto a fringe. Small rubber stamps are good for this, and you can print while the fringe is still on the frame, or after it has been taken off.

1 Using acrylic or fabric paint, press the rubber stamp firmly onto the wrapped yarns and leave to dry. You can outline the design using bottled paint to give more emphasis to the pattern.

2 Now steam the fringe thoroughly and remove it from the frame, as described on page 76.

It is possible to print a fringe after it has been eased or cut off the frame. This gives a much less ordered look, with just dabs of colour that relate to the same printed pattern that is on the embroidery.

FURTHER EXPERIMENTS

You might like to take this painting to extreme and dip the fringe into paper pulp, or paint the wrapped fringe thickly with emulsion paint, Xpandaprint (puff paint) or texture pastes.

Wrap the yarns on the frame, stitch down the centre or on one edge and take the fringe off the frame. Tie a length of yarn to one end and then paint it. Hang it up from a hook and then pull, twist and wiggle the loops until you have made the shape you want and leave it to dry. You will get paint all over your hands when you do this, so you might like to use rubber gloves.

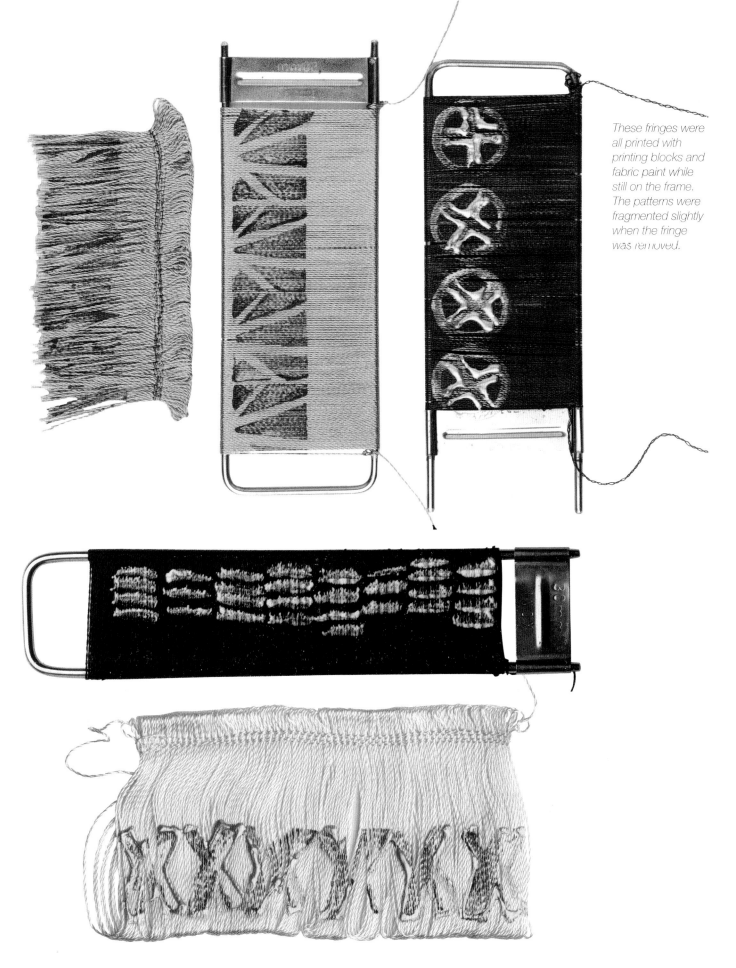

These fringes were all printed with printing blocks and fabric paint while still on the frame. The patterns were fragmented slightly when the fringe was removed.

4 CORDS AND BRAIDS

Zigzag cords

There are so many ways of making cords and braids using the sewing machine that you will never run out of ideas. One of the best known is to zigzag over a length of yarn or string, completely covering it. However, there are many possible variations on this basic method. Cords can be over-wrapped with wire, strips of fabric or paper, knotted, twisted on a cord winder, crocheted or plaited with two others. Think of the ways the ends can be treated by dipping them into gold paint, covered with beads, knotted, or the cord wrapped around small wooden moulds to give ends with some weight to them. These are especially good for hangings and bags.

Zigzag cords can be soft or stiff, thin or thick, and can also be used to couch onto an embroidery, woven through buttonholes or made into fringes or tassels. This can be a technique that you use frequently and so it is worth doing a number of samples to see what you can achieve.

A small book wrap made with layers of stitching, machine-made lace and beads. Zigzagged cords were threaded through holes in the spine, and knotted and beaded at the ends.

A very large tassel with pieces of embroidery edged with zigzag cord threaded through coiled wire. (Jacqui Brimacombe)

Machine-wrapped cords

This is a simple technique with a multitude of uses. Using zigzag stitch on your machine you can cover string, knitting yarns, embroidery threads, raffia, wire, strips of fabric or tights, knitting ribbon, or anything else you can find in your stash of oddments.

The cords can be used as edgings, ties, loops, to hang wall panels, to secure books, or you can use three to make a twisted cord, wrap the head of a tassel, or to couch onto an embroidery.

Method

Needle
Use a needle to fit the thread.

Top thread
Any machine embroidery thread will do, coloured or metallic.

Bobbin thread
This will show, so should match the top thread.

Tension
Normal or slightly loose.

Foot
You will get a much better result if you use a braiding foot, also called a knit edge foot, bulky overlock foot or pearls and piping foot, depending on the make of machine you have.

Teeth
These should be up.

Stitch
Use the widest possible zigzag stitch on your machine, even if you are covering a fine cord.

Stitch length
This should be about 3. If it is longer you will get an uneven cord, if it is shorter it will take you too long to cover.

1 Knot the ends of the cord and the threads together and hold them at the back of the foot. Then start stitching fairly slowly, holding the cord behind and in front of the needle. Do not pull, but just hold it so that it goes through in a straight line.

2 Do not try and cover your cord in one pass. For one thing, you will not be able to do it as neatly as you wish, and for another, your thread might break in the middle of the journey. When this happens, pull the cord away from the needle and cut the threads. Then start again, holding all four threads towards you, lying along the cord, so that they are covered as you stitch.

3 You can use a different colour on every journey, or you can use the same colour for the first couple of journeys and, when you have nearly covered the cord, change to a contrast colour or a metal thread for the final contrast.

To add texture
You can make bumps or 'beads' by moving the cord back and forth slightly, allowing the stitching to build up in one place.

You can also include small tufts of fabric or yarn as you stitch, holding them in place with an orange stick until they are secure.

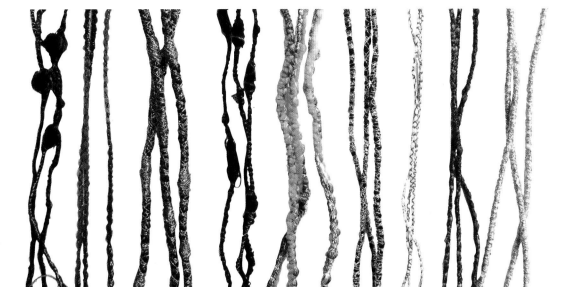

Left: Zigzagging a variety of yarns to make cords.

Below: A book wrap made of silk 'paper', tied with a zigzagged cord. Scraps of the silk paper were included in the stitching to give a soft effect.

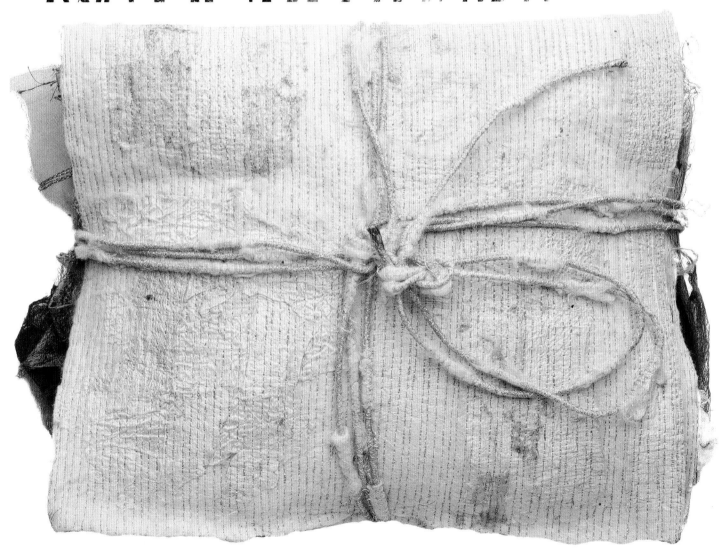

Spiralled cords

Once the cord has been made, extra strips of texture or pattern can be loosely coiled around it. Consider strings of beads, strips of painted nappy-liner or Tyvek zapped with a heat gun, strips of ragged stitched paper grids, frayed strips of fabric, long lines of automatic patterns stitched on the sewing machine, or textured yarns.

Spiralled cords, with loosely wrapped and attached scraps of paper (top), other cords and a strip of stitching (centre) and scraps of stitching worked on water-soluble fabric.

Method

1 Pin the end of a strip to one end of a zigzagged cord.

2 Zigzag for 2.5 cm (1 in) or so to hold it firmly in place.

3 Hold the strip away from the cord and zigzag down the cord for a short distance. Then coil the strip around the cord once (or twice) and zigzag it again to secure it.

Continue like this until the whole strip has been attached at intervals.

Cord ends

The ends of cords can be finished by wrapping them firmly with a contrast thread, dipping them in gold paint, adding a collar of beads, or by gluing the ends into a large bead. They can also be glued around a tassel mould to fit on the end of a rod supporting a hanging.

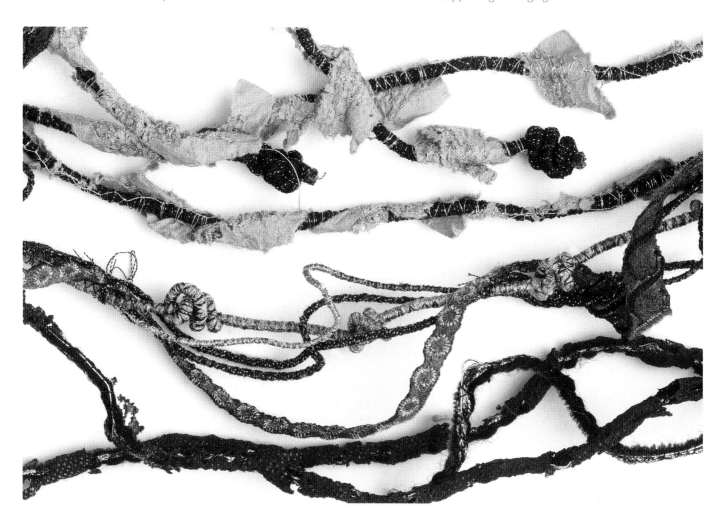

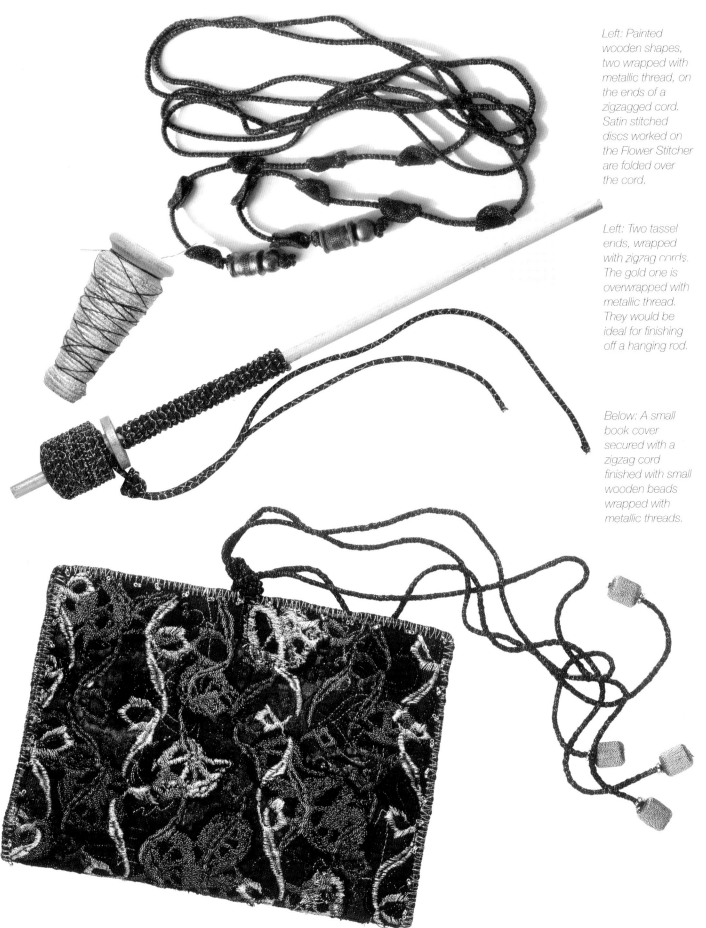

Left: Painted wooden shapes, two wrapped with metallic thread, on the ends of a zigzagged cord. Satin stitched discs worked on the Flower Stitcher are folded over the cord.

Left: Two tassel ends, wrapped with zigzag cords. The gold one is overwrapped with metallic thread. They would be ideal for finishing off a hanging rod.

Below: A small book cover secured with a zigzag cord finished with small wooden beads wrapped with metallic threads.

Beaded cord ends

A collar of beads makes a lovely finish for a cord, hiding the cut ends and adding shine and colour as well as some weight to make the cords hang properly. This is one of the few hand methods in this book, but is a good way to finish off a machine-made cord on books, bags or cushions.

Beaded book wrap with zigzagged cords with Peyote stitched ends. (Gill Morgan)

Make flat rectangles of beading and then sew them into a tube to slip onto the ends of the cord. I use peyote stitch but you could try square stitch instead.

Method

Beads
Use size 11 seed beads, or Delicas (anything larger looks clumsy).

Needle
Use a size 10 beading needle.

Thread
Nymo is one of the best to use as it is flat so will pass easily through the eye of a beading needle.

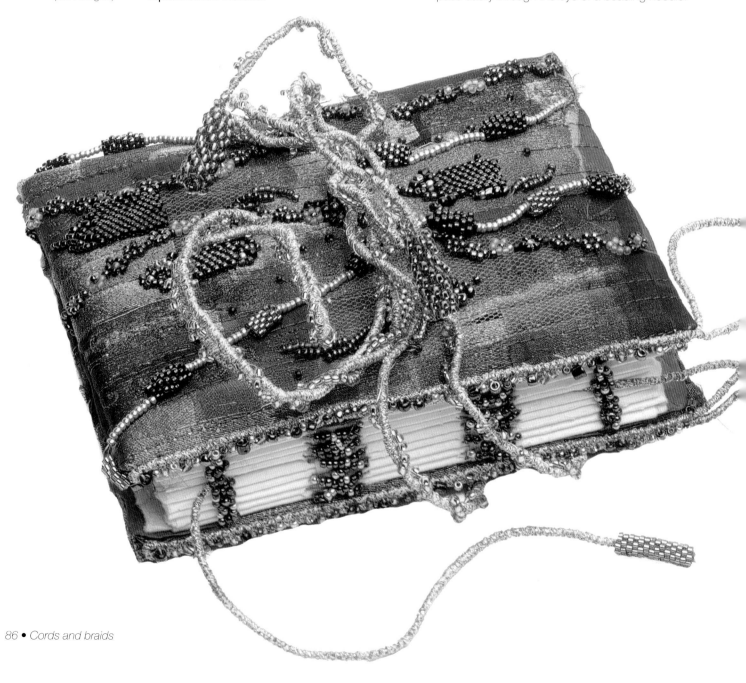

Flat peyote

a String a light-coloured bead on the thread and take the needle through it again leaving a 15 cm (6 in) tail. Add a dark bead, a light bead and another dark bead (diagram a).

b Pick up a dark bead and go through bead number 3, pulling the threads tight so that the beads make a T-shape at the end (diagram b).

c Pick up another dark bead and go through bead number 1. Pull the thread tight to make beads 2 and 4 pop up (diagram c).

Continue adding two light and two dark beads on alternate rows, making a flat rectangle of beads. Work an even number of rows leaving the threads coming from opposite corners.

d When you have worked a few rows, try wrapping the beading around the cord. It should be very tight. Join the beads together as in diagram d.

Showing how to make Peyote stitch tubes for the ends of cords.

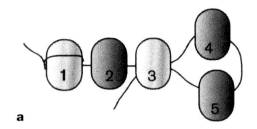

a

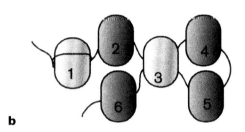

b

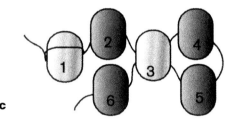

c

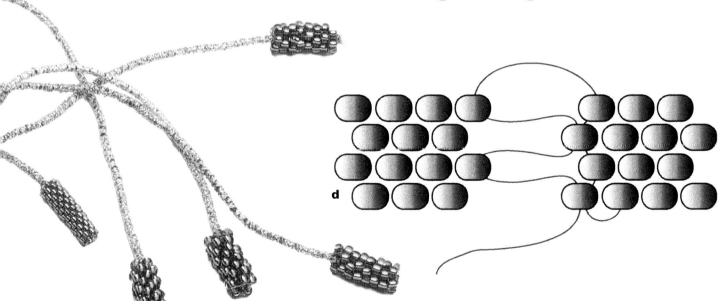

d

Knots

Knotting is one of the most useful techniques for finishing ends of cords, even when they are only simple overhand knots. They act as a stopper at the ends of cords. Trim the ragged ends close to the knot and add a dab of PVA to prevent them unravelling or coming undone.

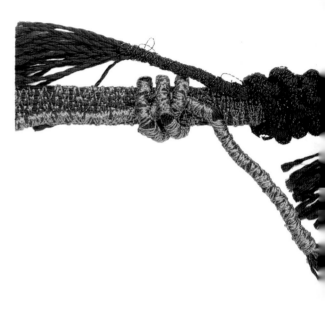

A slightly more complex knot, such as a double, treble or multiple overhand knot, is still simple to do and gives a larger knot with more weight. A couple of the best knot books are listed in the Bibliography on page 126, and these give directions for any other knots that you fancy. If you are already a knot expert you could try a Monkey's Fist or a Turk's Head.

Knots can also be used for tying things onto a cord, such as rings or beads, for tying short lengths of cord to another cord or braid, or for adding more texture along a length of cord.

Right: Overhand and multiple overhand knots.

Far right: A large multiple overhand knot.

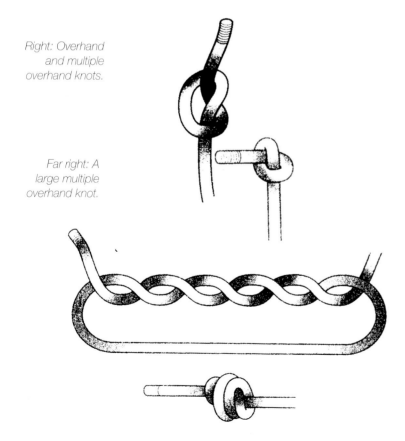

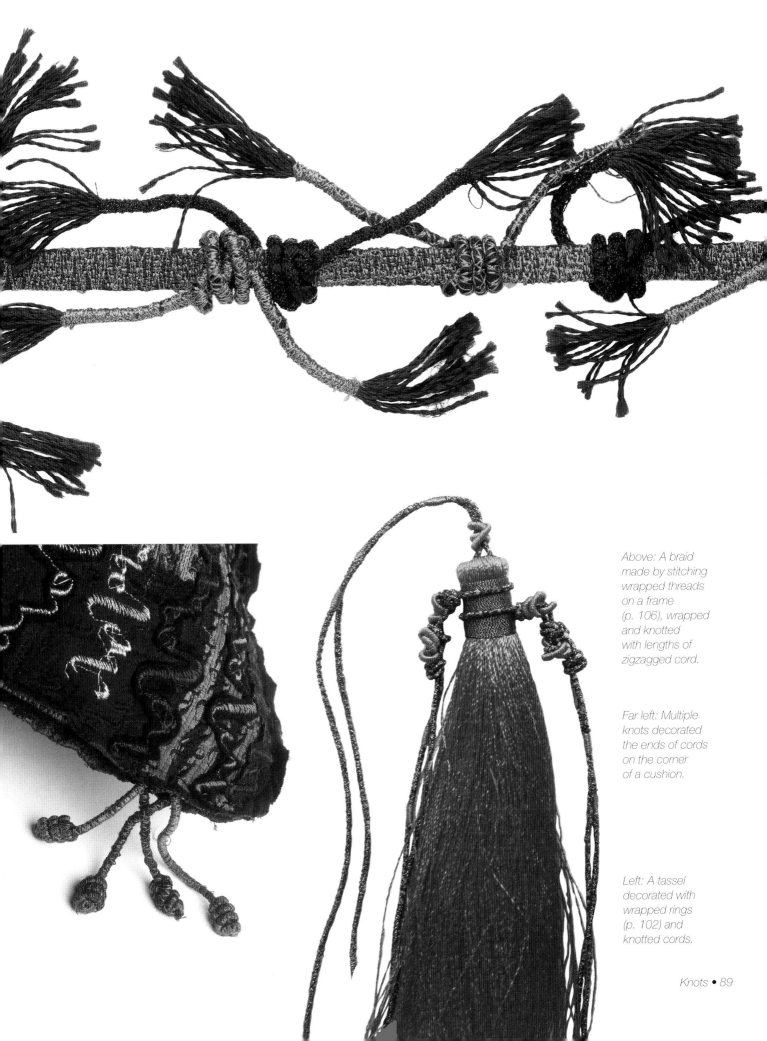

Above: A braid
made by stitching
wrapped threads
on a frame
(p. 106), wrapped
and knotted
with lengths of
zigzagged cord.

Far left: Multiple
knots decorated
the ends of cords
on the corner
of a cushion.

Left: A tassel
decorated with
wrapped rings
(p. 102) and
knotted cords.

Looped, twisted & doubled cords

Having zigzagged your cord you can then do more with it to make a larger, chunkier more textured cord.

The bottom three cords are crochet cords, or finger chains, made with zigzagged yarns. The top multiple cord includes knotting, wrapped rings, beads and metallic rings. These were threaded on before the chain was made and slipped onto some of the loops. The below one is made with a zigzagged cord buttonholed over another one.

Doubled cord

Hold two zigzagged cords together and join them with another row of zigzag stitching. Alternatively, you could use one of the utility stitches for this.

Twisted cord

Make a twisted cord using a pencil (the old method) or a cord winder (much easier and results in a more professional cord). Use contrasting colours if you wish to define the twist. You can twist three cords, or six for a larger, chunky cord.

Looped cord

Make a very long zigzagged cord and then use it to make a simple chain as you would in crochet. This is also called a finger cord, but the method is the same.

Make a slip knot in one end of the cord, leaving a loop. Pull another loop through it, tightening the loop as you go.

You can string on some wrapped rings, beads or metal tubes to add texture.

For even more texture you can use the zigzagged cord to make any of the simple macramé braids using buttonhole stitch or just interlacing

Left: Zigzagged cords twisted on a cord winder to make chunky, stiff cords.

Below: A book wrap secured with a doubled cord – two zigzagged cords stitched together to make a flat braid.

Stitched thread braids

Stitching threads, yarns and narrow ribbons together produces wonderful flat braids which can be machine stitched together to make wider ones, decorated on top, or folded to make chevrons. It is so satisfying to use up many threads or yarns that you have no use for, and to make something that is beautiful and useful for decorating and edging cushions, lampshades, chairs and stools, bags or clothes.

Opposite: Stitched thread braids, including simple, crocheted, decorated with automatic patterns, and threaded through separately stitched shapes.

Method

Needle
Use a needle to suit the top thread.

Threads
Use any fine threads such as stranded cotton, DMC perlé, crochet cotton, knitting or weaving yarns, fine knitting ribbon, novelty knitting yarns, fine raffia, twisted silks, and even metallic machine embroidery threads. Beware of the very stiff metallic cords as these are difficult to handle.

Top thread
Use a machine embroidery thread, coloured or metallic.

Bobbin thread
This will show, so use one that matches or co-ordinates with the top thread.

Tension
Normal.

Foot
Use the standard foot.

Teeth
These should be up.

Stitch
Choose a running stitch, 3-step zigzag or stretch stitch (it is the same thing but different manufacturers call it by different names). It usually comes directly next to the zigzag stitch.

Stitch width
Choose the widest stitch so that it completely covers the yarns.

Stitch length
About 1½.

Have a large plastic bowl under the table, between your feet, to hold the balls or hanks of yarn. Find four or five threads or yarns, drop them into the bowl and, making sure they run freely, knot them together at one end. Hold this knot behind the foot and start stitching. If you have too many threads for the stitching to cover, remove one.

Joining the braids
Hold two braids together and work the same stitch down the centre. Hold them lightly, because if you pull one even slightly, the braid will end up with a curve. If you continue to join a number of braids together, you can make a fabric.

Decorating the braids
You can couch a cord on one of these braids, stitch a satin stitch pattern on it, or apply previously stitched slips, patches or motifs.

Making stitched thread braids using the 3-step zigzag.

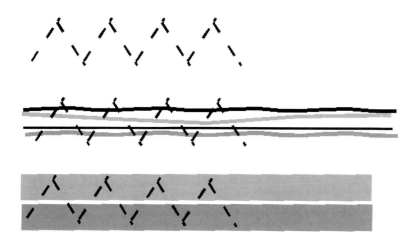

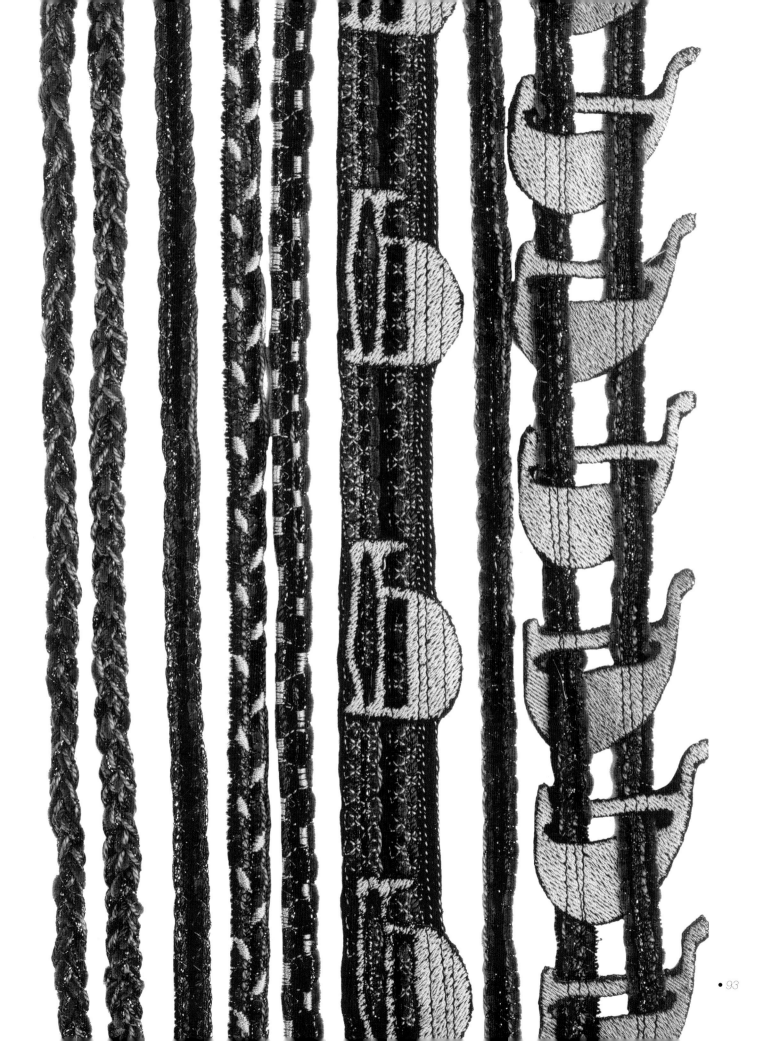

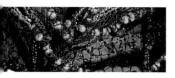

Zigzag crochet chain

Opposite: Vessel made from separate pieces of stiff embroidery edged with a crochet chain. (Margaret Curry-Jones)

This cord is made by first working a simple crochet chain and then machining over it. The stitching skips over the bumps in the chain, leaving knobs of colour showing between the stitching. It is a slightly more informal cord and adds texture to the edges.

Method

Chain

Start with double knitting wool, although you can later try the cord with knitting ribbons, two or three yarns worked together, or an embroidery thread such as stranded cotton or silk. Work a length of simple crochet chain or finger braid using a largish hook.

Then go to your machine to work the stitching.

Needle

Use a needle to fit the thread.

Top thread

Use machine embroidery thread, either coloured or metallic.

Bobbin thread

This will show, so match to the top thread.

Tension

Normal.

Foot

It is easier not to have a foot on the machine so that you can see better. If you need a foot, then use the one with a tunnel underneath called the braiding, knit edge or 'pearls and piping' foot.

Teeth

These should be down.

Stitch

Use zigzag, set at the widest your machine will allow.

Holding the chain behind as well as in front of the needle, work close zigzag between the bumps in the chain. In theory you can stitch evenly along the chain with the stitching sliding over the bumps. However, I find that I have to do it in short bursts, moving the chain along slightly whenever I reach a bump.

Right: Crochet chain cords made from double knitting wool, dishcloth cotton, a space dyed rayon yarn and some yarns and ribbons lightly zigzagged together, with a sample of one of them used as an edging.

Flower Stitcher braids

These braids were all made using zigzagged cords or stitched thread braids combined with satin stitch rings made using the Flower Stitcher. If you do not have one of these attachments, rings can be made using the software on your sewing machine, or stitched freehand. The easiest way to do this is to use a free running stitch and work a number of rows to fill the shape of a ring. It is extremely difficult to do a satin stitch ring freehand so I would not even try.

The rings were folded, coiled, twisted or laid in overlapping rows with a zigzag cord couched down the middle to hold them together. If you make a number of rings and a couple of cords, you can play and fiddle until you come up with something quite different from those shown here.

Method

Fabrics

Use felt, either a very thick one or a thinner one doubled, to give the rings more body.

Needle

Use a needle to fit the thread you are using.

Top thread

Use a machine embroidery thread, either coloured or metallic.* Variegated colours work well with this method as you will stitch the rings twice.

Bobbin thread

This is likely to show, so match the top thread.

Tension

Normal.

Foot

Attach the Flower Stitcher according to the manufacturer's instructions.

Teeth

These should be down. This is crucial, as the attachment will not work unless they are.

Stitch

Use zigzag stitch. The width should be the widest possible, but check that the needle does not hit the plastic ring of the Flower Stitcher by rotating the hand wheel very gently. You can also adjust the needle position, moving it to the left, which allows you to stitch a wider zigzag.

1 Work two rounds, the second one exactly on top of the first. This stiffens the rings, which is necessary for the braids. You can then remove the Flower Stitcher and stitch two or three circles on the outside and the inside of each ring.

2 Cut a hole in the centre, and then cut around the outside of the rings. Burning the edges over a nightlight gives the neatest edge and also helps to stiffen them slightly.

Right: a) Shows free running around a Flower Stitch ring. b) Cord woven through rings. c) A number of rings overlapped and stitched to make a formal braid.

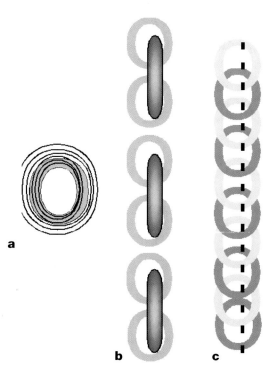

a

b

c

Left: A variety of
cords and braids
using Flower
Stitcher rings.

Below: A book
wrap decorated
with Flower
Stitcher rings
worked on felt and
water-soluble
fabric. The cord
has some rings
wrapped and
stitched on
each end.

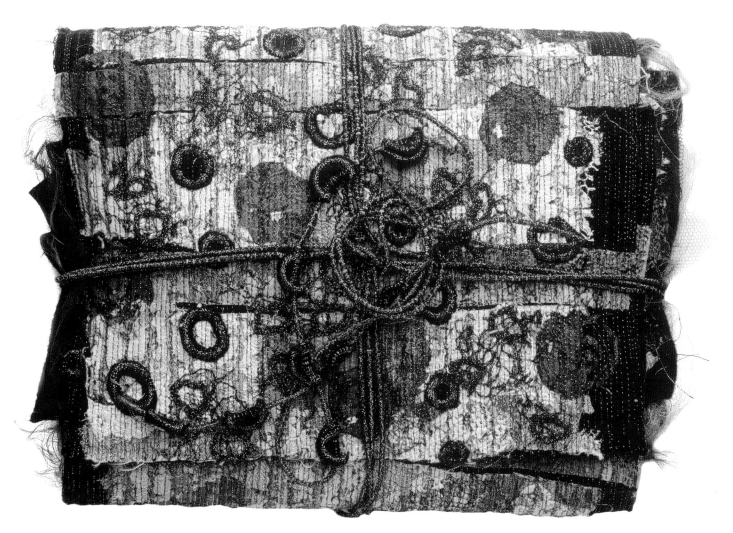

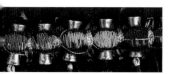

Patterned braids

The many patterns on modern sewing machines can be used alone, or combined with each other, to make handsome braids. Braids are usually pretty sturdy, so felt, or a sandwich of fabric bonded to felt, makes a good base and is easy to stitch.

The braid can be a single line of a satin stitch pattern, different patterns stitched next to each other, or a cut-out pattern stitched over the top of more patterns.

Holes can be stitched or burnt with a soldering iron with cords threaded through them, and beads added by hand for sparkle and colour.

Method

Some designs for wider braids using large automatic patterns over strips of fabric or ribbon, or threaded with cords.

Fabrics
Use felt or other sturdy fabric.

Needle
Size 90 or 100 is best for this.

Top thread
Use a machine embroidery thread, coloured or metallic.

Bobbin thread
Any coloured thread can be used, as it will not show.

Tension
Slightly loose top tension, normal on the bobbin.

Foot
Use the embroidery foot. This usually has wider toes so that you can see the pattern, and space under it so that the satin stitches are not squashed.

Stitch
Use any satin stitch patterns as these give richness.

Stitch length
Set for satin stitch.

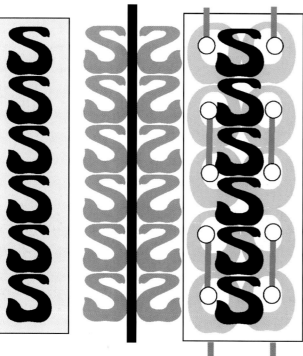

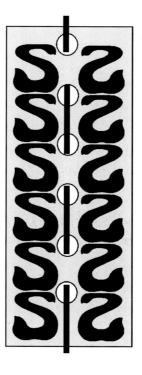

Left: Braids
decorated with
automatic patterns
and buttonholes
on felt.

Left: A fringe
headed with a
complex braid. A
row of a satin stitch
pattern was
worked on felt. A
second row of the
same pattern was
cut out and
applied over
dumbbell shaped
metallic beads.

Left: Braid made
using two layers of
acrylic felt, stitched
down the centre with
an automatic pattern.
It was slit at intervals
and burnt with a heat
gun. (Penny Usher)

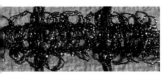

Braids on water-soluble fabric

Many of the automatic patterns can be stitched on water-soluble fabric to make filmy and less precise braids.

All the water-soluble fabrics on the market are good, but for braids use a hefty one that needs no frame. A lighter-weight fabric can be used double, but try a sample with your chosen stitch to see how it works.

Method

Fabrics
Use a heavy water-soluble fabric.

Needle
Size 90 or 100.

Top thread
Use a machine embroidery thread, coloured or metallic

Bobbin thread
The thread will show, so choose a toning or contrasting colour in your colour scheme.

Tension
Normal.

Foot
Use the embroidery foot. This usually has wider toes so that you can see the pattern, and space under it so that the satin stitches are not squashed.

Stitch
The lighter-weight stitch patterns are better for this method, at least for the first layer. A satin stitch pattern, or buttonholes, can be worked on top of this foundation.

The lines of stitching must overlap each other, otherwise the whole thing will fall apart when the fabric is dissolved. Work a sample first, and try overlapping them halfway, but results will depend on which stitch you use.

Ribbons
Narrow ribbons can be laid on the water-soluble fabric and the stitches worked over this, with more rows along each side.

Left: Building up automatic patterns in layers so the stitching is dense enough not to disintegrate when dissolved.

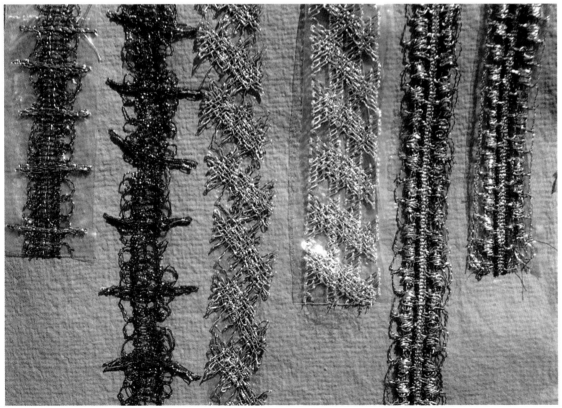

Left: Braids stitched on heavy water-soluble fabric, before and after dissolving them.

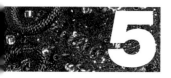

5 TASSELS

It is almost impossible to add too much decoration to a tassel, and beads, knots, looped cords, wrapping and extra pieces of embroidery can all be added to integrate the tassel with whatever it is attached to. It is essential to watch the proportions of a tassel. They can be short and fat, or long and thin. The neck can be wrapped for 0.5 cm (¹/₄ in) or even for 5 cm (2 in), depending on the look you want. The skirt can be short and bouncy, even almost non-existent, or very long indeed if you use the right yarn that hangs elegantly.Making simple tassels perfectly needs practice. They can be used alone, as an extra skirt around another tassel to give it bulk, or a number of them can be included in a fringe, or used as a base for machine-embroidered pieces. They do need to be designed along with the embroidery they are to decorate, and the same style, colour and threads used.Sometimes the technique used in the main embroidery can be developed to make a new type of tassel, and some of those methods are given in this chapter.

Wrapped rings

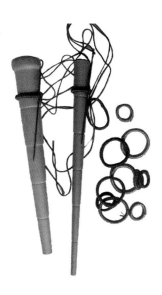

Making wrapped rings on a ring stick.

Many of the cords and tassels in this book include wrapped rings as part of the structure or decoration. Nearly all of the tassels illustrated here have a wrapped ring twisted around the cord at the top of the head to finish it off, or to keep a larger bead from sliding up the cord. They can be used to hang tassels from a fringe, to loop cords through, or just as a decorative edging as in the black tassel shown here.

Method

Most of the rings in this book are made on a ring-stick that measures 5 cm (2 in) in circumference around the widest part. A larger one can be looped, twisted or knotted if you wish.

1 Using a fairly fine yarn, wrap it around the top end of the stick so that the working thread comes from the left-hand side.

2 Wrap about 12 times. More wraps makes a thicker ring – you will have to experiment with the yarn you are using.

3 Leave approximately 75 cm (27 in) of yarn free, and cut the yarn. Thread it through the needle. Take a stitch up through part of the bundle of threads and pull.

4 Slide the needle down behind the wrapped yarn, pull the thread through and then pull it up, holding it on the top of the stick with your left forefinger. You must keep the yarn under tension to keep the ring tidy.

5 Repeat this, taking the yarn *behind* the wrapped threads every time and not *through* them, keeping the stitches as close together as you can.

6 To finish off, take a stitch through the ring backwards for about 0.5 cm (¹/₄ in). You may need to pull this through with some pliers. Cut the thread and slide the ring off the stick.

Making a tassel

Choose a suitable yarn – that is, one that hangs nicely. Also, the cut ends should not splay out untidily or the bottom of the skirt will look ragged. I find a silk or rayon yarn, or thick silk or rayon embroidery thread, or a fine chainette, is the best to use.

Method

1 Make a cord using any method you choose.

2 Wrap the yarn over a piece of card or a wire frame until it looks thick enough. Tie a loop of thread through half the yarn to stop it falling all over the place as you carefully ease it off the card.

3 Knot the ends of the cord inside the loop of yarn. Holding the cord up in the air, smooth the yarn over the knots to hide them.

4 Choose a textured metallic thread to wrap the neck with, as it will grip the tassel yarn and not slide off. Wrap the neck by laying the thread along the hank of yarn with the end down at the bottom. Start wrapping the neck just under the knots, covering the beginning of the thread as you go. Wrap very tightly for at least 0.5 cm (¼ in) to secure the tassel. Cut the metallic yarn and thread it in a needle. Slide the needle up underneath the wrapping, pull it tight and cut it off. Also cut off the first end of the metallic thread.

5 Cut the loops and trim them if you need to.

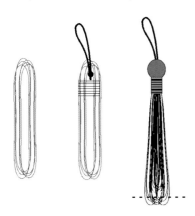

Above: The stages in making a simple tassel.

Far left: Some suitable proportions for a tassel.

Left: A richly stitched tassel head worked in layers, decorated with wrapped rings. (Anne Simpson)

Wire frame tassels

This is a quite different way of making very small tassels, using the same threads as you have used in your embroidery, and even some of the same stitchery or edgings. These tassels are made by machine stitching over the wrapped yarn to make a neck, which is then looped or knotted before the final wrapped finishing. They are quite small and so are suitable for small embroidered pieces.

Method

Frame
You will need a 10 or 12.5 cm (4 or 5 in) long frame made from wire, or you can make your own using wire coathangers and parcel tape. A 17.5 cm (7 in), 22.5 cm (9 in) or even longer frame can be used, and these will have longer necks that can be knotted or looped.

Yarns
Wrap the frame with a yarn that is thicker than your machine thread, or, if you cannot find one, use the same thread that you are stitching with. Tie the beginning of the thread onto the frame, wrap the yarn around the frame until it looks thick enough. Do not wrap too many times or your zigzag will not fit over it.

Needle
Use a size to fit the embroidery thread.

Top thread
Use a machine embroidery thread, coloured or metallic.

Bobbin thread
Use the same thread as the top thread.

Tension
Normal.

Foot
Do not use a foot at all, so that you can see what you are doing.

Teeth
Drop the teeth (feed dogs).

Stitch
Use the widest possible zigzag.

1 Start stitching 2.5 cm (1 in) from the end of the frame. This length can be varied according to the size of the frame and whether you wish to knot it. You will need about 6 cm (2½ in) of wrapped neck to tie a knot on a tassel made on a 22.5 cm (9 in) or longer, frame.

2 Work down to the other end, the same distance from the frame, zigzagging all the wrapped yarns together. You will need two or three journeys, as you did when zigzagging a cord (see page 94).

3 Finish by working a few straight stitches into the end of the wrapping.

4 Cut the loops of the yarn, fold the tassel in half, or knot it, and wrap the two ends together by hand. You can finish off the threads by sewing them into the wrapping.

Variations
You can wind some threaded beads around the neck before you finish off the tassel, or add rings.

- You can make two tassels exactly the same (count the wrappings and measure the stitching) and then use them together.

- Make a number of them and add them to a fringe.

Left: A wire frame wrapped with yarn and the neck stitched, with some finished tassels made using this method.

Left: A smaller frame also wrapped and stitched, with two tassels using the same method. The left tassel was made on a long frame, and the right tassels on a shorter one.

Wrapped ribbon tassels

These are similar to the wire frame tassels (pages 104-5) except that more yarn is wrapped around the wire frame and it is machined to and fro across the wraps to make a flat ribbon. As the first edges are not particularly beautiful, a separate stitched edge is added along the sides of the ribbon. Alternatively, tiny beads can be sewn along the edge before it is knotted, or stitched randomly all over the surface. An automatic satin stitch pattern can be worked down the centre of the ribbon.

A cord can be looped through the knot, or the tassel can be stitched onto an edge of an embroidered piece.

Method

Yarns
Rayon embroidery threads or fine rayon weaving or knitting yarn are all suitable.

Frame
Use a wire frame 22.5 by 7.5 cm (9 by 3 in). This can be made from an old wire coathanger or purchased (see the Suppliers' list on page 126) and can be longer if you wish.

Wider tassels decorated with extra stitching on the edge, one with beads and two enclosing metal rings in the knots.

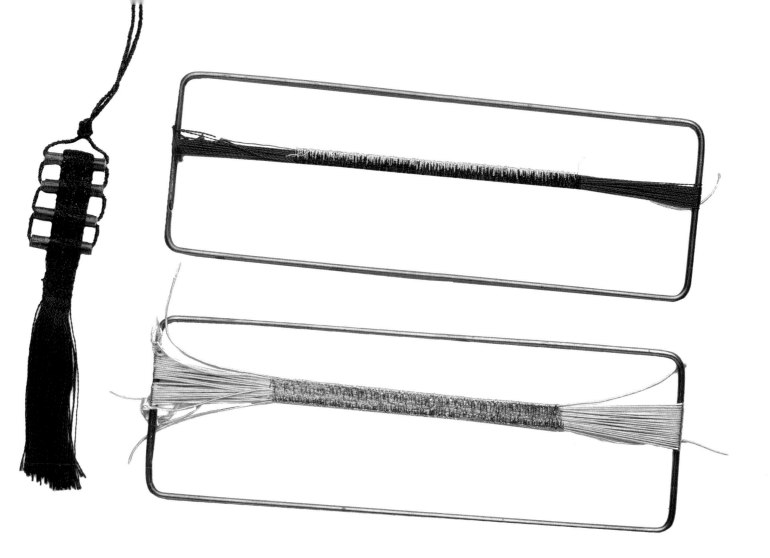

Needle

Size 90 or 100.

Top thread

Use a plain colour or variegated machine embroidery thread.

Bobbin thread

This will show, so use the same colour as the top thread.

Tension

Keep this at about 3.

Foot

Use a darning or free embroidery foot, or a quilting foot. Or you can take the foot off altogether.

Teeth

Drop the teeth (feed dogs).

Stitch

Set the machine to straight or running stitch.

Stitch length

You can ignore this as the teeth are lowered. If you cannot lower the teeth on your machine then try setting the stitch length to 0.

1 Tie one end of the thread or yarn to one end of the wire frame and wrap it around the frame, counting each complete wrap as one. If you are making a number of these tassels you will need to know how many turns you have made. Flatten it out with your fingers as you wrap until it looks about the right width for your purpose. Start with a width of about 1 cm ($^3/_8$ in) if you wish to make a small knotted tassel – you may have to experiment with the number of wraps depending on what thread you are using.

Above: Two ribbon tassels as they are made on the frame, and a finished tassel stitched over paper beads, laced with a zigzag cord.

Far right: A complex tassel made by combining a ribbon tassel, and wide and narrow zigzagged cords looped and wrapped around each other.

2 Lay the frame sideways under your machine needle, and stitch back and forth at right-angles to the yarns to hold them together in a flat ribbon. Start about 7.5 cm (3 in) away from one end of the frame and stitch to within 7.5 cm (3 in) of the other, then go back over it and stitch again for more firmness – maybe even a third time. The ribbon should be quite stiff. Press your foot pedal hard but move the frame slowly so that your stitches are nice and small and the ribbon is not distorted.

To edge the ribbon work *one* of the following:

- Satin stitch in a contrast colour or metallic thread.

- Lay a length of gimp or fine cord along one edge and satin stitch over it.

- Work a decorative satin stitch along the edge. Choose one that has one straight edge and keep this edge on the edge of the ribbon.

Cut the thread at each end along the wire frame, and knot it loosely in a simple overhand knot. Bring the ends of the stitching together and secure by hand or machine.

Rings or larger beads can be added if you can find the right shapes.

Right: Some of the possible edgings on a ribbon tassel: Gimp zigzagged on the edge. Long and short stitch (an automatic pattern) worked on the edge. Beads stitched on by hand.

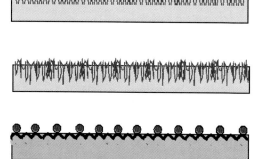

Wider ribbon tassels

These are made slightly differently from the wrapped ribbon tassels. They are wider and much softer, so when they are knotted they look like a strip of cloth.

Method

Yarns

Use rayon embroidery threads or fine rayon weaving or knitting yarn.

Frame

Work on a wire frame 38 cm (15 in) or longer by 8 cm (3 in). This can be made from an old wire coathanger or purchased (see the Suppliers' list on page 126) and can be longer if you wish.

Needle

Size 90 or 100.

Top thread

Use a plain colour or variegated machine embroidery thread.

Bobbin thread

This will show, so use the same colour as the top thread.

Tension

Keep this at about 3.

Foot

Use a darning or free embroidery foot, or a quilting foot. Or you can take the foot off altogether.

Teeth

Drop the teeth (feed dogs).

Stitch

Set the machine to straight or running stitch.

Stitch length

You can ignore this as the teeth are lowered. If you cannot lower the teeth on your machine then try setting the stitch length to 0.

1 Tie one end of the thread or yarn to one end of the wire frame and wrap it around the frame, counting each complete wrap as one. Start with a width of about 2.5 or 3 cm (1 or 1¼ in).

2 Lay the frame sideways under your machine needle, and stitch back and forth at right-angles to the yarns to hold them together in a flat ribbon. Start about 7.5 cm (3 in) away from one end of the frame and stitch to within 7.5 cm (3 in) of the other. Leave narrow spaces between the lines of stitching. The ribbon should be quite soft.

3 Cut the ribbon off the frame and knot it. A single overhand knot will be all you can manage with a shorter frame, but you can tie two or three if you use a 5 cm (2 in) frame.

A wider ribbon tassel, knotted twice and with a hanging fish bead.

Hanging tassels

These tassels are made of shapes sewn onto water-soluble fabric, and then only partly dissolved so that they remain very stiff. They are formed into three-dimensional shapes while wet and allowed to dry slowly. Then the pieces are strung together or sewn to a cord to make a small tassel.

Method

Fabrics
Use heavyweight cold water-soluble fabric (often called Romeo).

Frame
Use a ring frame.

Needle
Size 90.

Top thread
Use a coloured machine embroidery thread.

Bobbin thread
This can be matching or contrasting in colour, but it will show.

Templates with graduated shapes used for making these tassels.

Tension
Normal.

Foot
Use the free embroidery foot, or no foot at all.

Teeth
Drop the teeth (feed dogs).

Stitch
Straight stitch.

You can use a square, round, oval or triangular shape for these tassels, and they must get progressively smaller. A long rectangle can be twisted around a stick to make a helix, and a number of these can be grouped together. Drawing office templates like those shown here are the best, and you will need about nine different sizes of a single shape, stitching two of each size. You could also design these shapes on your computer if you do not have a template.

1 Draw the shapes onto the water-soluble fabric using a felt pen in a similar colour to the thread you are using.

2 Stitch right around the edge of each shape, and then across it horizontally, with lines of stitching quite close together, catching in the stitched edge.

3 Then work the same stitching in the other direction, and a third layer in the first direction again. The stitching should be quite thick. You could work an edging here if you wish, perhaps in a different colour.

4 Cut the stitching away from the fabric, and soak the pieces in warm water. As soon as the fabric turns to a jelly, take them out, peeling the jelly away from the edges.

5 Form the pieces into shapes and leave to dry.

6 Thread the shapes from the smallest to the largest, with a bead in between to space them out, and make a beaded loop on the top.

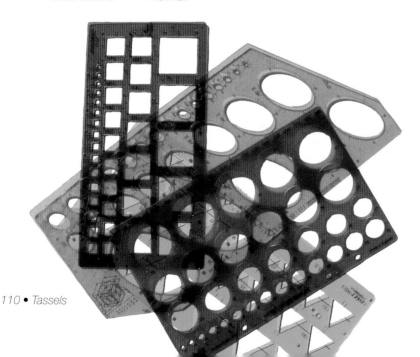

Left: Three hanging tassels made from a number of graduated shapes. (The right-hand tassel is from Janet Crowther.)

Left: Small hanging tassels can be used to decorate the skirt of a large tassel.

Below: Some of the shapes that can be produced with solid stitching on water-soluble fabric.

Stylised tassels

If you own a top-of-the-range sewing machine, you will have some larger motifs either built in, or on extra cards, or designed on the computer. A number of these can be stitched onto firm fabric and sewn together to make interesting tassel tops. If you do not have one of these machines then you can stitch some motifs using free embroidery. If you have a Janome 9000 with its scanner, or a Bernina Deco with its scanner, you can scan in your drawing and the machine will stitch them for you.

Method

Fabrics
Use a firm cotton or silk, backed with felt.

Frame
Fit the embroidery bed and frame to your machine, or use a ring frame.

A few of the patterns on Bernina and Pfaff cards that can be used to make tassel heads.

Needle
Size 90 or 100.

Top thread.
Use a coloured or metallic machine embroidery thread.

Bobbin thread
Match this to the colour of the felt backing.

Tension
Normal or slightly loose.

Foot
Use the free embroidery foot.

Teeth
Drop the teeth (feed dogs).

Stitch
This will be set by the machine, or you can use a combination of stitches if you are doing free embroidery.

1 If you are doing free embroidery, draw the design onto your fabric.

2 Frame the fabrics tightly.

3 Stitch your chosen motif.

4 Make a cord and a tassel, wrapping the neck firmly.

5 Cut the motif away from the background, and singe the edges if they need it. This does help to stiffen the motif.

6 Wrap one, two or three motifs around the head and stitch them firmly to it.

Pinch and tuck

These tassels are decorated with simple geometric shapes, firmly stitched to give body. Each piece is edged with more stitching and then pinched and stitched through folds to give organic and floral shapes. The diagrams are marked to show how to stitch each shape, but hold a piece in your hand and fold and pinch it to give different results. This manipulation becomes quite addictive after a while, and it is a challenge to see how many different shapes you can make from a square, for example.

Make a card template, or use commercial templates such as the easily obtained patchwork templates. The size of the shape will be determined by the size of the tassel you wish to make, but start with the sizes given on the diagram.

Method

Fabrics
Use either a single layer of felt, which could have a fine fabric placed over it, or two layers of net, or two layers of net and a layer of a transparent fabric.

Frame
Use a ring frame.

Needle
Use a large needle, size 100, or a special embroidery needle.

Top thread
Thread two machine embroidery threads through the needle. Try using a variegated thread and a metallic one. Using two threads together adds interest and covers the fabric better.

Bobbin thread
Use one thread in the bobbin, to match the fabric colour.

Tension
Loosen your top tension, as using two threads together will automatically tighten it. Tension 1 gives a nice-looking stitch on the back, which is often more attractive than the stitching on the front.

Foot
Use a darning or free embroidery foot, or a quilting foot. Or you can take the foot off altogether.

Teeth
Drop the teeth (feed dogs).

Stitch
Set the machine to straight or running stitch.

Stitch length
You can ignore this as the teeth are lowered. If you cannot lower the teeth on your machine then try setting the stitch length to 0.

1 Draw around the template onto your fabric, using a coloured pencil or a water- or air-erasable pen, and place the fabric in a ring or hoop.

2 Stitch small overlapping circles, completely filling the inside of the shape. Move the frame slowly, keeping your foot pressed hard down on the pedal so that the stitches are quite small.

3 Then stitch spaced circles around the outside edge of the fabric, going twice around each circle for strength.

4 Cut the stitching away from the background and singe the edges in a frame close to the stitching. If you are using synthetic fabrics you could cut the shape out with a soldering iron, but this is virtually impossible to do on fabrics made from natural fibres.

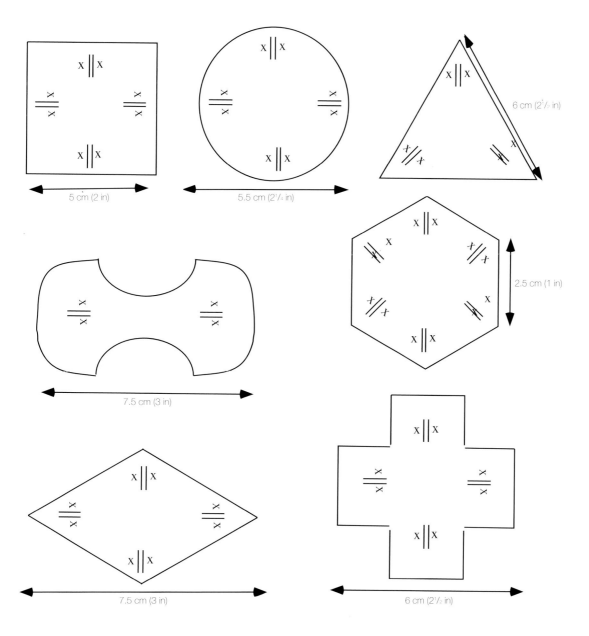

Left: These shapes
can be used as
patterns for Pinch
and Tuck tassels.

5 cm (2 in)

5.5 cm (2¼ in)

6 cm (2⅜ in)

2.5 cm (1 in)

7.5 cm (3 in)

7.5 cm (3 in)

6 cm (2½ in)

Left: Some of the
commercial
templates that can
also be used.

Far right: Some of the pinched and tucked shapes that can be used to make tassels.

5 Decide which side of the stitching you wish to show most of, and then pinch folds on the back (see diagrams). Hand-stitch firmly for about 0.5 cm (¹/₄ in) to hold the fold in place. You may need to then turn the piece over and push the centre up or down to give the effect you want.

6 Try bringing the points together, laying one piece on top of another or placing two of the same shape back to back, and perhaps sewing them together around the edges and stuffing them.

7 If you wish to layer these pieces on a tassel cord, then make a hole in the centre of each piece with a stiletto large enough to pull the cord through.

Right: Free running in random loops built up in layers to cover the fabric. The pieces are then edged with more loops.

Opposite left: The flat shapes were heavily stitched and then built up in layers. The bottom piece was stitched to the neck to make this flower-like shape.

Opposite right: A flower tassel made using the method on p. 155. (Gwen Soomre)

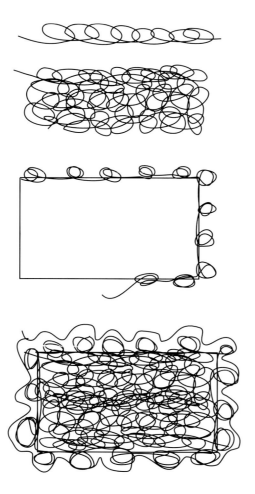

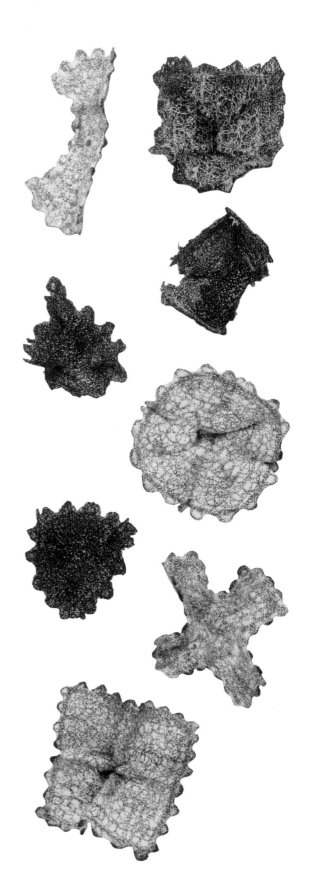

Folded tassels

5 cm (2 in)

10 cm (4 in)

10 cm (4 in)

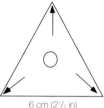

6 cm (2½ in)

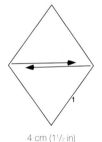

4 cm (1½ in)

The geometric shapes which can be folded in different ways to make tassel heads.

These tassels are a development of the pinch and tuck tassels, equally firmly stitched but formed into much more geometric shapes. They can be folded into cubes, cones or pyramids, and the edges burnt, or decorated with stitching or beads.

Make a card template, or use commercial templates such as the easily obtained patchwork templates. The size of the shape will be determined by the size of the tassel you wish to make, but start with the sizes given on the diagram.

Method

Fabrics

Use either a single layer of felt, which could have a fine fabric placed over it, or two layers of net, or two layers of net and a layer of transparent fabric. Make a hole in the centre of the shape using a stiletto and do not stitch across it – this is for the cord to go through.

Frame

Use a ring frame.

Needle

Use a large needle, size 100, or a special embroidery needle.

Top thread

Thread two machine embroidery threads through the needle. Try using a variegated thread and a metallic one. Using two threads together adds interest and covers the fabric better.

Bobbin thread

One thread in the bobbin to match the fabric colour.

Tension

Loosen your top tension, as using two threads together will automatically tighten it. Tension 1 gives a nice-looking stitch on the back, which is often more attractive than the stitching on the front.

Foot

Use a darning or free embroidery foot, or a quilting foot. Or you can take the foot off altogether.

Teeth

Drop the teeth (feed dogs).

Stitch

Set the machine to straight or running stitch.

Stitch length

You can ignore this as the teeth are lowered. If you cannot lower the teeth on your machine, try setting the stitch length to 0.

1 Draw around the template onto your fabric, using a coloured pencil or a water- or air-erasable pen, and place the fabric in a ring or hoop.

2 Stitch back and forth as in the diagrams, completely filling the inside of the shape. Move the frame slowly and keep your foot pressed hard down on the pedal so that the stitches are quite small.

3 Cut the stitching away from the background and singe the edges in a frame close to the stitching. If you are using synthetic fabrics you could cut the shape out with a soldering iron, but this is virtually impossible to do on fabrics made from natural fibres.

4 Decide which side of the stitching you wish to show most of, and then fold them to make three-dimensional shapes. Hand-stitch firmly for about 0.5 cm (¼ in) to hold the fold in place.

Far left: A tassel using a number of folded squares. (Lynn Horniblow)

5 cm (2 in)

Left: The stitching leaves voided lines that will be slit afterwards, and then folded.

4 cm (1½ in)

Below: Folded tassels using half a hexagon, a square, a square and a diamond.

5 cm (2 in)

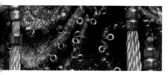

Wavy tassels

These tassels are yet another development of the pinch and tuck tassels, equally firmly stitched but distorted in a different manner. The central holes are larger, and when the stitching is finished a small ring is stitched inside the hole. The ring is too big for the hole and this distorts the whole shape.

Method

Fabrics

Use a single layer of felt, which could have a fine fabric placed over it. Cut a hole in the centre of the shape and do not stitch across it.

Frame

Use a ring frame.

Needle

Use a large needle, size 100, or a special embroidery needle.

Top thread

Thread two machine embroidery threads through the needle. Try using a variegated thread and a metallic one. Using two threads together adds interest and covers the fabric better.

Bobbin thread

Use one thread in the bobbin to match the fabric colour.

Tension

Loosen your top tension, as using two threads together will automatically tighten it. Tension 1 gives a nice-looking stitch on the back, which is often more attractive than the stitching on the front if you have used different colours.

Sewing a ring into a square or circular hole to distort the shape.

Foot

Use a darning or free embroidery foot, or a quilting foot. Or you can take the foot off altogether.

Teeth

Drop the teeth (feed dogs).

Stitch

Set the machine to straight or running stitch.

Stitch length

You can ignore this, as the teeth are lowered. If you cannot lower the teeth on your machine, try setting the stitch length to 0.

1 Make a card template of a circle or a square. The size of the shape will be determined by the size of the tassel you wish to make, but start with one that is about 3 cm (1¼ in) along each side of the square, or a circle with a diameter of about 5–6 cm (2–2½ in).

2 Draw around the template onto your fabric, using a coloured pencil or a water- or air-erasable pen, and stitch back and forth, radiating the stitches from the centre, or filling in each section separately. You can add further decoration on top using narrow satin stitch.

3 Cut the stitching away from the background and singe the edges close to the stitching. Holding the ring inside the hole, stitch by hand according to the diagram, pulling the stitches tight to distort the shape into waves. Decorate the edges with tiny beads.

4 When you have made a number of these pieces, thread them onto a tassel cord with beads between each acting as spacers if you wish.

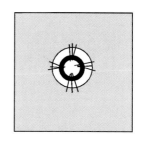 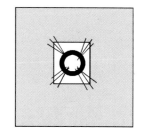

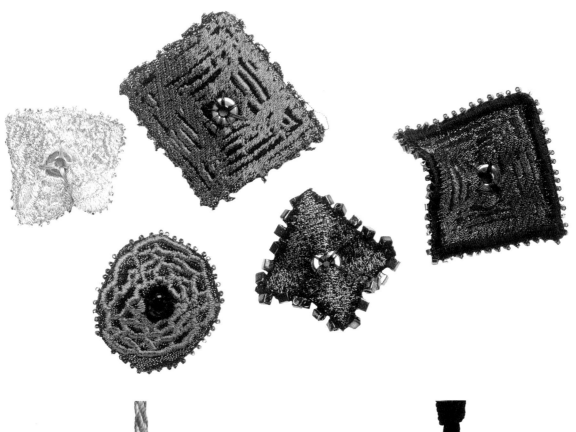

Left: The stitched and distorted shapes that can be used to make wavy tassels.

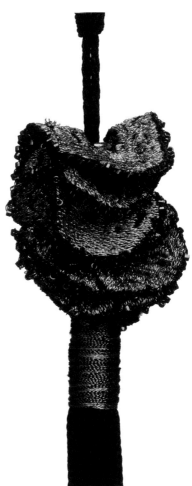

Left: Wavy tassels made with a number of stitched and distorted circular shapes, edged with beads, and piled up to give interesting tassel heads.

Flower tassels

This tassel is much larger than any of the others in this book, each one being about 25 cm (10 in) long and 10 cm (4 in) wide. They are a combination of a number of techniques: zigzag cord, firmly stitched and shaped flowers, fringes stitched on net using automatic patterns, more flowers, knotted cords, finished off with tassel-shaped beads at the bottom of the skirt and a bead and wrapped ring at the top. You can add your own variations to the basic method as you go along.

First make the cord, about 50–60 cm (20–24 in) long.

Then make the basic tassel. The sample shown here (page 103) was made of black knitting wool to make it bouncy. You can of course change the colour scheme entirely.

Then work the fringes, make more cord for the skirt, and finally make all the flowers.

Method

Templates for this flower tassel.

FOR THE FRINGES

Fabrics
Use black net, doubled.

Frame
This is not needed.

Needle
Size 90 or 100.

Top thread
Gold machine embroidery thread.

Bobbin thread
Black.

Tension
Slightly loose, maybe 2¹/₂.

Foot
Use the standard foot.

Teeth
These should be up.

Stitch
Find an automatic pattern of small leaves or flowers.

Stitch length
This will be set by your machine.

1 Stitch lines of pattern about 20 cm (8 in) long on the doubled net. There should be seven or eight lines, worked slightly apart from each other.

2 Cut away from the net, close to the stitching.

3 Attach to the neck of the tassel at equal intervals apart.

4 Then sew a bead on the bottom to give weight so that they hang well.

METHOD FOR THE KNOTTED CORDS

1 Work a zigzag cord about 1 metre (1 yard) long, depending on how many knots you wish to tie.

2 Knot it at 2.5 cm (1 in) intervals or less, and then cut into 20 cm (8 in) lengths.

3 Attach to the neck between the fringes.

METHOD FOR THE SMALL FLOWERS ON THE FRINGE

Make a thin card template of the small flower pattern, slightly less then 2.5 cm (1 in) across.

Fabrics
Use black felt.

Frame
Use a ring frame if you need one.

Needle
Size 90 or 100.

Top thread
Gold machine embroidery thread.

Bobbin thread
Black.

Tension
About 2½, depending on your machine.

Foot
Use the darning, quilting or free embroidery foot.

Teeth
These should be down.

Stitch
Free running.

1 Draw around the flower template onto the felt. You will need three flowers for each hanging fringe – more if you wish.

2 Stitch the flowers according to the diagram, working enough rows so that they are quite stiff.

Above: Stitching pattern for the petals.

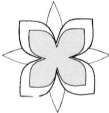

Above: Building up the pieces of stitching in layers to make flowers.

Left: A tassel for a special occasion made with stitched petals, hanging fringes, extra simple tassels and beads.

3 Cut out the flowers and singe the edges in a candle flame.

4 Sew them at intervals onto the fringes.

METHOD FOR THE LARGE FLOWERS

Below: All the pieces necessary to make this grand tassel.

1 Make two card templates for the double flowers, or three for the treble flowers. The thin petalled template will measure 7.5 cm (3 in) across, the smaller flower about 4 cm (1½ in) and the larger flower about 5 cm (2 in) across.

2 Stitch them in the same manner as the small flowers. You will need four of each size.

METHOD FOR THE THIN TASSELS

Use a fine rayon or silky thread for these. They should be about 22.5 cm (9 in) long. Make four tassels to hang on a fine thread instead of a cord. Thread each one through a suitable bead.

PUTTING IT ALL TOGETHER

1 Assemble the flowers by sewing the rounded petals in front of the spiky ones. For the tassel shown opposite, the back of the stitched spiky petals gives a darker tone to the flowers. Sew the flowers to the neck so that the petals stick up.

2 Sew a beaded tassel to the middle of each flower.

3 Finally, pull the cord through a larger bead, and twist a wrapped ring around the cord to secure the bead. You may need to go shopping to find the beads you need for this tassel, unless you already have a good stock of large beads.

Conclusion

I do hope this book gets you excited about some different ways of finishing your embroideries. A really well-designed edging, cord, fringe or tassel can enhance the whole piece, while a badly designed one can ruin it. Take at least as long to think about the finishings as you have about the main part of the embroidery, and you will have endless pleasure every time you look at it.

Suppliers and bibliography

Sewing machines

Bernina, Bogod Machine Co Ltd,
50–52 Great Sutton Street,
London EC4 0DJ.
Brother, Shepley Street, Audenshaw,
Manchester M34 5JD.

Husqvarna/Pfaff, Husqvarna Viking House,
Cheddar Business Park, Wedmoor Road,
Cheddar, Somerset BS27 3EB.
Janome Centre, Southside, Bredbury,
Stockport, Cheshire SK6 2SP.

Equipment and materials

The suppliers below do mail order – ask for
a catalogue.

Art Van Go, 16 Hollybush Lane, Datchworth,
Knebworth, Herts SG3 6RE. (Art supplies)
Franklin's, 13/15 St Botolphs Street,
Colchester, Essex CO2 7DU.
(Flower Stitcher)
Lynn Horniblow, Sparacre House, St Andrew's
Road, Bridport, Dorset DT6 3BB.
(Wire tassel frames, ring sticks and tassel
moulds)
Rainbow Silks, 6 Wheelers Yard, High Street,
Great Missenden, Bucks HP16 0AL.
(Fabrics, paints, Bondaweb, 505)
Strata, Oronsay, Misbourne Avenue, Chaltont St
Peter, Bucks SL9 0PF.
(Xpandaprint (puff paint), chiffons)
Scientific Wire Co., 18 Raven Road, London
E18 1HW. (Coloured copper wire)

FABRICS
Fabric Land, Silver Business Park, Airfield Way,
Christchurch, Dorset BH23 3TA.
(Acrylic felt and good choice of reasonably
priced fabrics and haberdashery)
Whaleys (Bradford) Ltd, Harris Court Road,
Great Horton, Bradford, West Yorkshire
BD7 4EQ.

THREADS
William Hall & Co., 177 Stanley Road, Cheadle
Hulme, Cheadle, Cheshire SK8 6RF.
(Folded viscose rayon yarns – 1200/2 is the
one to ask for)
Handweavers' Studio, 29 Haroldstone Road,
London E17 7AN. (Rayon yarn for tassels – ask
for colour samples)
Silken Strands, 20 Y Rhos, Bangor LL57 2LT.
(A vast range of machine embroidery
threads)

Bibliography

Beaded Tassels, Braids & Fringes,
Valerie Campbell-Harding, Sterling, 1999.
0-8069-4891-4
***The Complete Guide to Knots and Knot
Tying,*** Geoffrey Budworth, Lorenz Books,
1999. 0-7548-0422-4
Encyclopedia of Needlework,
Thérèse de Dillmont,
DMC Library.

Giving Pleasure, Jan Beaney & Jean Littlejohn,
Double Trouble, 2001.
0-9531750-7-3
The Handbook of Knots, Des Pawson, Dorling
Kindersley, 1998. 0-7513-0536-7
Patterns of Fashion, *1560–1620*, Janet Arnold,
Macmillan, 1985.
The Tassel Book, Anna Crutchley, Lorenz
Books, 1996. 1-85967 222 1

A sample of many fabric edges including, from top to bottom: painting, Prairie Points, cut and rolled tabs, fraying, loopy stitching, appliqué diamonds, couching and more fraying. (Ruby Lever)

INDEX

WITHDRAWN

Right: A velvet flower, each petal edged with random zigzag over fine wire. (Beryl Watts)